WILLIE MORRIS

Shifting Interludes

SELECTED ESSAYS
EDITED BY JACK BALES

UNIVERSITY PRESS OF MISSISSIPPI • *Jackson*

The following essays were previously published in:

"As the Years Go By, Do We Grow Crankier—Or More Tolerant?" *New Choices: Living Even Better After 50*, April 1996; "At Ole Miss: Echoes of a Civil War's Last Battle," *Time*, 4 October 1982; "Bridgehampton: The Sounds and the Silences," *New York Times*, 1 March 1974; "Capote Remembered," *Homecomings*, Jackson: University Press of Mississippi, 1989; "Coming on Back," *Life*, June 1981; "Despair in Mississippi; Hope in Texas," *Dissent*, Summer 1963; "Down South We Fry Them on the Sidewalks," with Ed Yoder, *The Isis* (Oxford University), 22 May 1957; "Eisenhower," *The Isis* (Oxford University), 27 February 1957; "The Epistolary Soldier," *Texas Observer*, 18 May 1990; "Here Lies My Heart," *Esquire*, June 1990; "In a Shifting Interlude," *American Way*, 15 September 1991; "In the Spirit of the Game," *Southern Living*, November 1990 (originally published as "The South" in *Game Day USA: NCAA College Football*, 1990), © Southern Living, Inc.; "It Took More Than Good Men to Win the War," *Washington Star*, 12 February 1976; "The John Foster Dulles," *Car and Driver*, November 1992; "A Love That Transcends Sadness," *Parade*, 13 September 1981; "Mississippi Queen," *Vanity Fair*, May 1999; "Mississippi Rebel on a Texas Campus," *The Nation*, 24 March 1956; "Mitch and the Infield Fly Rule," *Homecomings*, Jackson: University Press of Mississippi, 1989; "My Friend Forrest Gump," *Oxford American*, March/April 1995; "My Friend Marcus Dupree," *Parade*, 30 October 1983; "Now That I Am Fifty," *Parade*, 21 April 1985; "Of Northern Fears, Southern Realities, and Jimmy Carter," *New York Times*, 8 July 1976; "Prelude to Setting Off in a Camper to History," *Washington Star*, 17 February 1976; "The Rain Fell Noiselessly," *Texas Observer*, 22 August 1958; "The Round-Up," *Daily Texan* (University of Texas at Austin), 23 February 1955; "The Round-Up," *Daily Texan* (University of Texas at Austin), 7 June 1955; "The South and Welcome to It: Does It Still Exist?" *Southern Magazine*, October 1986; "Southern Comforter," *New York Times*, 10 August 1973; "Weep No More, My Lady," *Reader's Digest*, October 1974; "What It Takes for a Son to Understand a Father," *Parade*, 26 August 1984.

www.upress.state.ms.us

10 09 08 07 06 05 04 03 02   4 3 2 1
∞

Library of Congress Cataloging-in-Publication Data

Morris, Willie.
    Shifting interludes : selected essays / Willie Morris ; edited by Jack Bales.
        p.   cm.
    ISBN 1-57806-478-3 (alk. paper)
    I. Bales, Jack.   II. Title.

PS3563.O8745 S55 2002
814'.54—dc21   2002022974

British Library Cataloging-in-Publication Data available

CONTENTS

Coming on Back

INTRODUCTION

On an unseasonably mild summer afternoon in 1998, Willie Morris and I left his tree-shaded house on a quiet street in Jackson, Mississippi, for the hour-long drive to his hometown Yazoo City. "My town is the place which shaped me into the creature I am now," he frequently acknowledged in the course of his far-reaching career, and when I visited him, he proudly took me on his self-styled "$64,000 tour" of the place of his youth.

I don't know which one of us enjoyed the day more. As a researcher of his life and works, I was thrilled to participate in his journey through the past, though I was not surprised at his invitation. For throughout our visits, letters, and phone conversations, I discovered (as have countless others) that Willie had an unlimited capacity for kindness and generosity—his "great sweetness" was how intimate friends privately described it. And he, a patient guide despite my persistent questions, was clearly delighted at my boyish enthusiasm and interest.

Although I was indeed fortunate to have this interview with Willie, a person need not travel to Mississippi to trace the roots of one of the South's most respected writers. In the mid-1990s Willie had transferred his reminiscences to the pages of his book *My Dog Skip*. He decided to write these recollections because he felt emotionally drained after completing his 1993 *New York Days*, an autobiographical account of his frenetic and controversial years at *Harper's*. He wanted to relax by writing something just for pleasure. "And what's more fun," he often asked, "than the dog of your boyhood?"

The dog of Willie's boyhood in the early 1940s was Skip, an English smooth-haired fox terrier that his parents bought for him when he was nine. Skip could play football, run errands, sprint the 100-yard dash in 7.8 seconds, and even drive a car (with a little help). But this bestseller—

which many dog owners asked Willie to autograph to their pets—is more than just a bittersweet tribute to the canine companion of his youth. It is also a memoir of a bygone era of Saturday morning matinees, cane-pole fishing, Nehi sodas, and Fourth-of-July political rallies in a World War II–era small southern town.

While Willie drove me along virtually every street and road in his childhood community, he would talk about these formative years, reminisce about family and friends, and point out sites both personal and historical. *Here,* I thought, *is one contented man.* And as we turned onto one of Yazoo City's main avenues so he could show me the house in which he grew up—and Skip's grave in the backyard—I impulsively commented on how fulfilling his life as an author must be. "Well, Jack," he nodded, "I couldn't live without writing, and I have no alternative to words. Besides," he shrugged, "I can't do anything else."

But he *did*, as countless readers and admirers can attest. While a senior at Yazoo City High School he not only edited the school's newspaper, but he also excelled in baseball and basketball, worked part time for the local radio station as a disc jockey and sports announcer, was voted "most likely to succeed" by his classmates, and graduated class valedictorian in 1952. As the crusading, fiery young editor of the *Daily Texan* at the University of Texas in Austin, he fought the university administration over censorship, segregation, and other campus-wide controversies. Upon his Phi Beta Kappa graduation in 1956, he studied history at Oxford University as a Rhodes Scholar. From 1960 to 1962, as the no-holds-barred editor of the *Texas Observer*, a weekly political newspaper that supported human rights issues, he courageously reported events that the mainstream press seldom bothered to cover, such as illiteracy, racial discrimination, and the inequities of the death penalty.

In 1967 Willie became editor-in-chief of *Harper's*, shortly before the publication of his first autobiography, the widely acclaimed *North Toward Home*. As the youngest editor in the history of America's oldest magazine, he aggressively transformed the stodgy, lackluster publication into one of the country's most exciting periodicals. Such success notwithstanding, he eventually became embroiled in editorial disputes with the publication's owner and resigned in 1971 (a move that prompted the resignations of most of the magazine's chief contributing authors).

Following his departure from *Harper's* and a painful divorce, Willie moved to Long Island and began concentrating on his own writing. The next few years were productive ones as he published *Yazoo: Integration in a Deep-Southern Town* (1971); his classic story for children, *Good Old Boy: A Delta Boyhood* (1971); a novel, *The Last of the Southern Girls* (1973); the narrative for *A Southern Album* (1975); his reminiscence *James Jones: A Friendship* (1978); and dozens of magazine and newspaper articles.

By 1980 Willie was back in his native state as writer-in-residence and instructor in the University of Mississippi's English department. He continued writing, and the Ole Miss years saw the publication of the multi-layered *The Courting of Marcus Dupree* (1983), the children's book *Good Old Boy and the Witch of Yazoo* (1989), and several books of essays, including *Terrains of the Heart and Other Essays on Home* (1981), *Always Stand in Against the Curve and Other Sports Stories* (1983), and the award-winning *Homecomings* (1989). He also found time to encourage aspiring young authors. For instance, soon after a young University of Mississippi law student sat in on some of Willie's classes, he began writing his first novel and asked the writer-in-residence for advice, which was quickly given. Willie subsequently wrote a blurb for the book's dust jacket, praising John Grisham's *A Time to Kill* (1989) as "a powerful courtroom drama" and "a compelling tale of a small southern town searching for itself."

In 1990 Willie married JoAnne Prichard (editor of *Homecomings*), and they moved to Jackson where he wrote his triumphant *New York Days* (1993). *My Dog Skip* followed a couple of years later and after that *The Ghosts of Medgar Evers* (1998), in which Willie chronicles the story of the famed civil rights leader.

Shortly after the publication of this latter volume, a motion picture production company began filming *My Dog Skip*. Although Yazoo City had changed so much over the years that much of the movie was filmed in nearby Canton, Willie was pleased with the results and found the shooting during the spring and early summer of 1998 to be especially poignant. "It was déjà vu of the most stunning kind," he told me as we left Yazoo City for Canton, to see actors and actresses playing him, his parents, and his childhood friends. As the two of us meandered around the small town, he observed that it retained the anachronistic features he deemed essential for filming, such as antebellum mansions, a square with storefront awnings, and a venerable, carefully preserved county courthouse. "I'm grateful," he later commented, "that the producers paid zealous attention to the spirit of those years in making the details authentic."

After I returned to my home in Virginia, he wrote me often about the movie's progress. On August 1, 1999, he telephoned to say that he and JoAnne had just returned from New York where they viewed a preliminary screening. "*My Dog Skip* is by any measure an absolute classic," he wrote me later that evening, "and I *know* you'll love it. Come here for the premiere. I miss talking with you."

The next afternoon I received another phone call, this one informing me that Willie had suffered a heart attack earlier in the day. He died that evening, and I immediately made plans to travel once again to Mississippi.

During that first week of August, lengthy obituaries across the country praised the sixty-four-year-old writer's literary accomplishments as well as his generosity of spirit and affection for the South. As broadcast journalist and author Bill Moyers prophetically remarked in the mid-1980s: "In the end it will be the quality of his life that is the real contribution Willie . . . made to our times." The sixth-generation Mississippian became the first writer in Mississippi history to lie in state in the rotunda of the Old Capitol in Jackson. He was buried in Yazoo City's Glenwood Cemetery just thirteen paces from the grave of the Witch of Yazoo, the legendary character he immortalized in *Good Old Boy*.

But Willie, at his writing desk literally to the day he died, ensured that readers would continue to enjoy his books. Released just a few months after his passing, *My Cat Spit McGee* (1999) is both a sentimental and funny chronicle of the author's conversion from a longtime "dog man" to an unabashed cat lover. In *My Mississippi* (2000), a joint project between him and his son, photojournalist David Rae Morris, he examines "the snarled confluence of [Mississippi's] past and present" as well as its promise for the future. For Willie, home was always his native state, and he drew a great deal from his boyhood memories while writing *Taps* (2001), a coming-of-age novel of small-town southern life during the Korean War.

In the course of his literary career, Willie Morris attained national prominence as a journalist, nonfiction writer, novelist, autobiographer, and news commentator. In addition, he was also recognized as a master essayist. Soon after I discovered his books in 1995, I began tracking down the articles he wrote for magazines and newspapers, even going so far as to page through the hundreds of issues of the *Daily Texan* and *Texas Observer* to which he had contributed pieces.

I sent many of these decades-old clippings to Willie, who occasionally admitted that he had either misplaced his own copies of the articles or had forgotten he had even written them. As he related the circumstances behind his writings, he would suggest other avenues of research. "Sometime when we're together," he wrote in August 1996, "let's sit down and I'll prod my memory on magazine pieces I've written over the years which you may not know about." As we made plans to collaborate on a book of his essays, I began in earnest to pore over both literary indexes and his extensive collection of personal papers and manuscripts in the University of Mississippi's Department of Archives and Special Collections. Soon after I sent him two articles from *Parade* magazine, he wrote back: "I do want to come out with another essay collection in a year or so with essays not yet published in books. I hope you'll remind me to include the ones on fathers and sons and on cemeteries and death that you just sent me."

Willie's own untimely death precluded me from reminding him, although "What It Takes for a Son to Understand a Father" and "A Love That Transcends Sadness" are so skillfully written I doubt that he would have needed any prompting from me to include them in this book. We agreed to intersperse thoughtful works such as these two with ones of a lighter, often humorous nature, for instance, Willie's buoyant "The John Foster Dulles." A few pieces we added because they feature his opinions on national issues, such as "Southern Comforter" in the *New York Times*. On the other hand, an example of an article that displays his regional voice is the sobering "At Ole Miss: Echoes of a Civil War's Last Battle" that *Time* magazine asked him to write. Some essays, such as "Despair in Mississippi; Hope in Texas," reveal Willie's passionate absorption in social issues, for he often echoed William Faulkner's belief that the best writing focuses on "the problems of the human heart in conflict with itself." When Willie was elected editor-in-chief of the *Daily Texan* in

1955, he anticipated a few conflicts of his own. In the editorial debut that June of his regular column, "The Round-Up," he both introduced himself to his readers and cautioned them: "What about the editor? You have a right to know something about the man who will provoke sneers and censures and perhaps a few smiles during the next twelve months. Most important, he is a strong believer in a free, unhindered press. The Yankees threw his great-grandfather's presses in the town well in 1863, and he hasn't forgotten it."

Of the approximately seven hundred articles that I had collected, Willie and I selected about ninety that illustrate his precision and eloquence in crafting short compositions. In the summer of 2001 I pared the list to thirty-two. This resulting book is the largest published collection of his essays and is the first to include works that cover virtually his entire writing career—from his junior year in college to the year he died. *Shifting Interludes*, which might well be subtitled *The Best of Willie Morris*, represents another lasting volume to his rich literary legacy.

And speaking of legacies, just how will Willie Morris be remembered? In 1998, after he came to Virginia to visit me and to speak at Mary Washington College, a group of students who attended one of the sessions enthusiastically commented on his whimsical sense of humor and immediate rapport with his diverse audience. One student remarked in an e-mail discussion group that he did not know what to expect from the public lecture, but "within, oh, thirty seconds Willie Morris showed how endearing and funny a fellow he could be."

The word *endearing* has been used many times. A self-described "good ole boy," Willie—with his genial, adventurous spirit and self-effacing nature—captivated both friends and perfect strangers. When you were with Willie Morris, you felt that you were with your best friend, even if you had just met him fifteen minutes earlier. He inspired countless people, particularly those in the creative arts. "I am not so much involved in an organizational way in cultural events," he told me during a formal interview in 1997, "but I try to encourage young people in this regard."

Willie will be remembered as the voice of the South in general and of Mississippi in particular. In June 1999, readers of Jackson's *Clarion-Ledger* newspaper selected him as Mississippi's favorite nonfiction author of the millennium. Willie's southern roots and enduring love of home are evident in "Coming on Back," the appropriately named piece he wrote for *Life* magazine in 1981: "If it is true that a writer's world is shaped by the experience of childhood and adolescence, then returning at long last to the scenes of those experiences, remembering them anew and living among their changing heartbeats, gives him . . . the primary pulses and shocks he cannot afford to lose." Willie's writing reflected those changing heartbeats. "And," observed his wife JoAnne Prichard Morris in a recent interview, "no heart was bigger than Willie's."

This collection of articles is fashioned around several of the images that he often returned to in his literary works: people, places, and memories. The essays span the years 1955 to 1999 and include two previously unpublished pieces ("A Long-ago Rendezvous with Alger Hiss" and "The Day I Followed the Mayor around Town") and the first article he ever wrote for a national publication ("Mississippi Rebel on a Texas Campus").

Shifting Interludes is the only Willie Morris anthology not compiled around one central theme, as I selected essays that capture the ideas and beliefs that touched (no, *consumed*) him all his life: loyalty to family, friends, and home, the power of land, a mindfulness of the past, the texture of daily living in a small town, the glory and disappointment of sports, the unquestioning love of a dog, the complexities of race relations, and the fragility of human life. The varied works encompass biographical profiles, newspaper opinion/editorials, humor sketches, political analyses, travel pieces, a book review, sports commentaries, and, of course, his thoughts—both critical and affectionate—about his beloved Mississippi.

The essays show, for the first time in print, Willie's whole range of emotions. In these pages you will find him writing with melancholy as he recounts a visit to Yazoo City in "The Rain Fell Noiselessly," with grace as he salutes a college football team and its fallen comrade in "In the Spirit of the Game," with humor as he admits to a bout of middle-age infatuation in "Mitch and the Infield Fly Rule," and with pensiveness as he remembers his much-loved grandmother Mamie in "Weep No More, My Lady." But above all, you will always find him writing with candor, and it will always be right from the heart.

As Willie wrote so many fine essays, selecting the most appropriate ones for this volume proved to be a difficult task. I wish to thank Seetha Srinivasan, my editor at the University Press of Mississippi, for her assistance and characteristically astute advice. I also appreciate the input of Willie Morris's wife, JoAnne Prichard Morris, and his son, David Rae Morris. I am grateful to Edwin Yoder, Willie's longtime friend, for permission to reprint "Down South We Fry Them on the Sidewalks," the article they co-authored while at Oxford University. I also wish to thank the editors of the publications in which most of these essays originally appeared. Faculty and staff at Mary Washington College have always supported me in my writing endeavors, and I am pleased to acknowledge William M. Anderson, Jr., Carla Bailey, Ron Comer, William B. Crawley, Jr., Beth Perkins, Beverley Shelesky, and Roy Strohl, as well as members of the college library's reference staff. Other individuals who helped me include Dick Bales, Phyllis Bales, Steven L. Davis, Donald R. Eldred, John E. Ellzey, Jennifer Ford, Mary Grattan, Benjamin Hewitt, Larry L. King, Lisa K. Speer, and Thomas M. Verich.

Jack Bales
Mary Washington College Library
November 2001

*Weep No More,
My Lady*

Eisenhower

Back in late summer, some weeks after President Eisenhower had suffered his attack of ileitis, a few of the boys in the Washington press gallery spawned a mock release for clandestine consumption:

> The President died to-day at 3.15 and four seconds . . . President Assistant Sherman Adams reports that doctors have examined Mr. Eisenhower and find him contented and well-rested. The death, Mr. Adams says, has not altered the President's plans to seek re-election. Mr. Adams points out that there is no clause in the American Constitution restricting a dead man from running for President. "He would have wanted it that way."

The American people may not have relished the idea of a dead man in the White House, although it is common knowledge that they have stumbled in the wake of quite their share of public relations rococo. But the very fact that a man who had in no measure been a great or even an industrious President during his first term could carry the nation in '56 by the most impressive majority in history, might at least suggest that the corpse could have taken New England, a few states in the Midwest, and California.

He is the very quintessence of what the mid-century American would like to be. He is brave, affable, warm, sincere, gregarious, fair-minded, and honest. He is not an intellectual, and is seldom given to contemplation (as witnessed by his unwritten speeches and phrase-making); these, too, are part of the quintessent American. He has endowed Americans with a belief that no trouble exists with which he cannot cope, a simple faith recorded in the most widely-circulated smile since Greta Garbo's. He has given to America the kind of American confidence which belonged to Scott Fitzgerald's Dick Diver: "the illusions of a nation . . . of generations of frontier mothers who had to croon falsely to their children that there were no wolves at the cabin door." And in the process of being a President who wants more than anything else to be exemplary, he has become the most popular chief executive since Teddy Roosevelt.

The institution of the American Presidency has been gaining in influence and prestige throughout its history. For the most part this has been an evolution, nourished and embellished by a concomitant movement toward national unity. But it was the undercurrent of revolution which moulded the modern Presidency into its contemporary breadth. In the thirties, when the vigorous personality of F. D. R. played upon the exigencies of the times, the office assumed such extra dimensions as to produce fundamental pressures, still felt, on the half-shibboleth of federalism. But Roosevelt, for all those who respected him, was a viciously hated man: the very sweep of his social programme was enough to make bitter foes. Nor was his successor, Truman, an eminently popular President. With all his homely courage, he was too partisan, too brusque, to become any figure of national devotion. Then came Eisenhower, owner of the first mild, noncontroversial, Presidential personality since the office-moulding New Deal. As a soldier, he had already endeared himself to the public. When he took office, the mechanism for national worship was there: the press conference, the slick magazine, radio and television, the whole new substructure of precedented executive authority. All of these things had given rise to a national temperment which engendered a profound willingness to accept the man in the White House as something rather near to a constitutional monarch. F. D. R. and Truman, though they shaped the instrument and trained the temperament, could never quite fit into the symbolic role themselves. But Eisenhower has done so, and in a domestic age of manna and peace, he has reaped the harvests of the Presidential evolution.

There has been a strange air of immunity surrounding the man. If his administration errs, the blame invariably is fixed on the subordinate: a Nixon, a Dulles, Wilson, or Benson, whose verbal acrobatics have at least given a gamy flavour to an otherwise quiescent four years. Even in the international context, if my conversations with Englishmen hold any substance, it seems clear that abroad there are few positive or negative opinions about Eisenhower himself. Most of the vitriol is reserved for Dulles.

I have suggested that Eisenhower is the ultimate projection of the American dream. He is also the supreme product of the American moment. It is the moment of a burgeoning economy, which has glossed over the incongruent edges and encouraged a relatively quiet, complacent age. The fundamental tenets of the welfare state are firmly rooted, and the dominant national character is one of security, peace, and plenty. The fifties can rather be likened to the twenties in opulence and prosperity, lacking, however, the flaming colour and frosty exuberance. For the young generation (which is a more thoroughly Republican young generation than any of its recent predecessors) the present scene, as David Reisman has said, holds "neither fear nor fascination." Being a moderate in an age of moderation, Eisenhower has seen fit to bring only a moderate influence to bear upon domestic issues, and only in rare instances has he exerted his executive influence on Congress. In much the same perspective, he has delegated Presidential responsibility more than any other President; some say this is the soldier in him. Those politicians and theorists most concerned with his performance are quick to say that he does not control the office, but rather that the office controls him. Lacking the industry of a Truman or the intellectual depth of a Roosevelt, his concept of the executive seems to approach more nearly the Hoover-Coolidge brand of the twenties.

Of course, one must realize that he has another term before him, and that an assortment of possibilities are not to be discounted. One must also recognize the promising strides he has made in pressing upon America its responsibilities in the new internationalism. And before an observer can set forth any categorical opinion that Eisenhower has been a weak and harmless President, he should look more closely at the ensuing four years, to see how successfully he tries to use his influence on such vexing problems as the Middle East, segregation, education, and the whole fabric of executive-legislative relations.

In his prouder moments, Ike speaks the idiom of international love and world peace in his own simple, Wilsonian fervour. In his least proud moments he is a fumbling, uninformed man, riding the portentous crest of party expediency and national prosperity, shunning controversy for the sake of its shunning. I think it germane to note here that history has traditionally been suspicious of popular Presidents. Historians have probed beneath the façade of a moment and asked if such Presidents fostered devotion simply because they were uncontroversial, and were uncontroversial simply because they were too willing to fit their actions into the stereotype of a national mood. With his contemporaries, Eisenhower stands much closer to being a national myth than a Lincoln, or a Jackson, or a Roosevelt ever hoped to be in their own day. Perhaps this signifies that the nation stands to profit from an occasional gentle Presidency. But the very fact that Lincoln, Jackson, and Roosevelt have arrived at that elusive ever-ever land of American mythology after having suffered such hate and disrespect might suggest two theses: either Ike has one hell of a head start on posterity, or he will fizzle before he gets there: a pale shadow of an age that wanted a common denominator.

Down South We Fry Them on the Sidewalks

. . . He's too smart. We don't need a smart man for president. We need somebody to get things done . . .
> —Overheard in an Austin, Texas, barber shop, August 14, 1956.

You can be "too smart" to win the Presidency of the U.S.A., yet become part of its political legend, Adlai Stevenson has found. Not since President Warren G. Harding (a cigar-smoking, semi-literate Republican Senator who preferred a backroom poker game of a Saturday night to high affairs of state, and who pled for a return to "normalcy") has a candidate so indelibly written a word into the lexicon. Stevenson's word, of course, was "egghead." Nor been embarrassed during a campaign because his Dalmation stole across a fence and ate his neighbour's chickens. Nor become famous for the holes in his shoe soles. All these things did befall Adlai, and if he has run true to form he has squeezed every drop of humour out of them.

Stevenson has an affinity for improbable situations which makes him as fascinating in private as in public. He has distinguished himself—as governor of the State of Illinois, as a speechmaker who models his style after that of his fellow Illinois citizen, Abraham Lincoln, and the Biblical Book of Proverbs; as a raconteur. He likes to tell stories on himself. E.g.: about the woman who lost a diamond ring during a Democratic fund shortage and found she had last noticed it when she reached into Adlai's car to shake hands with him.

It is above all the "egghead" label which sticks. It all started in 1952 when the Alsop brothers' *New York Herald Tribune* column observed that even with the eggheads on his side he would have a tough time winning the presidency. Adlai retored: "Eggheads unite; you have nothing to lose but your yolks," and Americans long used to the parched diet of U.S. political talk sat up with a start. Stevenson was not scorning a staunchly lowbrow bent in American politics, so much as he was flashing the keen wit which is so much a part of him, yet which may have hurt him. Republicans quickly claimed that he was only a jokester, hardly to be taken seriously; voters who did not comprehend his wit distrusted it; others used the label "intellectual" as a scare word when they spoke of him.

The power of dogma is great, and the abuse of his wit by political enemies worked. But it is noteworthy that an analysis of his style showed—because he *is* a good prose writer—that it was far more comprehensible than Mr. Eisenhower's. The syllable count was lower; the concrete images thicker. He adhered closely to anecdotes and pithy illustration, while avoiding the gaseous and meaningless abstractions which for some reason are thought by Mr. Average American Voter to be "easier" to understand than good plain, simple—yet trenchant—English. If his wit is a part of Stevenson, so is his concern for the integrity of words and ideas; and it was one of those exasperating twists of American politics that the very fact made his "eggheadism" a liability.

As a politician, Stevenson strikes a rather marked contrast with his Democratic predecessor, Harry Truman, who received his honorary degree here last spring. Truman was a hard-hitting, brusque campaigner, crude and yet lovable in a homemade way. With little formal education, he served his apprenticeship in the stormy political wars of Missouri. His was the story of a Continent, and Americans like to tell themselves that their national lore is well-stocked with his kind. Those who met him here last June were impressed by his provincial's reverence of Oxford, and of the degree he was to receive. Stevenson, on the other hand, is much closer to the British political tradition. Educated at Princeton, Harvard, and Northwestern, he has relied to a great extent on intellectuals for counsel and support. The generalisation has been bandied and exaggerated, of course, but it is nonetheless true that the American temperament has always been such as to suspect the well-educated man in public affairs, particularly if, through some failing of his own, he sometimes shows it. Harold Laski, for instance, in his study *The American Democracy*, observed, "Despite the remarkable opportunities for higher education in the

United States, the man who can claim to have educated himself starts with a significant advantage over the man whose path to the university has been the result of parental care. . . . It is the uncommon man of common stock who reaches the places of importance."

In this respect, Stevenson and his 1956 running partner, Sen. Estes Kefauver, were no doubt the most oddly-matched political duo in half a century. Kefauver is a confirmed man of the people, a quaint mixture of professional gregariousness and rural absurdity. "I'm Estes Kefauver, and I'd like you to vote for me," was his trademark, as he walked down streets, through parks, across airport runways, calmly shaking hands with the faceless thousands. He, too, is an Ivy Leaguer (Yale Law School), but he prefers to hide the truth, and he does so at a moment's whim: by donning coonskin caps, or Indian head-dresses, or racing off kangaroo-style on a pogo stick. "What do you think of Elvis Presley, Mr. Stevenson?" a reporter asked, as Stevenson and Kefauver were mounting a plane last October. "Who's he?" Stevenson replied. "Why he's a good old Tennessee boy," said Estes, "and we're all mighty proud of him down here."

Stevenson's political future after his overwhelming loss to Dwight Eisenhower last November (he carried only seven states, six of them Southern) is very much in doubt. In all likelihood, the Democrats will not accept him again in 1960. Indeed, only one man in American history, William Jennings Bryan, has sought the Presidency again after two successive defeats. The kind of strategy his Party will surely use in the next election will be a we-need-a-change approach; it will be wary of gambling on a man who has twice before had his chance against the Republicans, and been soundly defeated both times. But there has been a great deal of speculation among Democrats—no small measure of it among the American colony at Oxford, which has traditionally been strongly Democratic—that in the event of a Party victory in '60, Stevenson might conceivably be appointed secretary-of-state. The idea seems a good one: he has worked in the UN, knows international law, travelled widely, and has long been observant of the contemporary world. And he has that sweep of imagination, that touch of sensitivity, that grasp of the American mission (with an accompanying trace of dislike for those foreign-service Americans most like the quiet one in Graham Greene's novel) that might well equip him to rank among the greatest.

Southern Comforter

BRIDGEHAMPTON, N.Y.—When I left the magazine business in the city a couple of years ago and came out here to live and work, I believed I had lost forever my sense of outrage. I felt that never again, after all my years in politics and public affairs, could anything ever evoke in me a feeling of indignation. I sensed that I had given too much of my flesh, and that something in me was destroyed and gone. But the exchanges between Senator Sam and Mr. Ehrlichman reaffirmed the contours of my own existence, and of my own past, and made me mad.

A neighbor of mine out here on the South Fork says over whisky that all Southerners go home sooner or later, even if it's in a coffin. Senator Sam has taken me home. A very large part of my youth and young manhood was devoted to politics in the South, sometimes to doom and lost causes, yet we were close to the earth even in our tempestuous disagreements, and never once did I allow myself to forget that my people founded my home state of Mississippi, that they were soldiers and editors and writers and, also, politicians, and that my great-uncle was a United States Senator who defeated Jefferson Davis for Governor of Mississippi in 1851.

Just before the Watergate hearings, I was on a radio program, where a New Englander said that he had just read the list of United States Senators who were to form the committee, and that he feared there would be a whitewash. He feared there were too many Southerners on the committee.

I suggested that he might be proven wrong. I told him that I had been on the opposite end of many fights with the old Southern conservatives, but that after all it was their people who had largely founded this nation, the laws and ethos of it, that they would be at their best on the profound constitutional issues now before the country, that they had fought a war and lost it on that document, and that they would do proud the better instincts of the whole society not only because of this, but because the criminal activities and grievous disregards of the Watergate group were an affront to their dignity and their professionalism.

I smile when I look at Senator Sam. He reminds me of my grandfathers and my uncles. He makes me miss them in their graves. I took the daughters of the Senator Sams to debutante balls and Saturday night picture shows a generation ago in the Mississippi delta. He talks in the accents and phrases of my boyhood. He helps me remember. He was formed by all the good substances of a place that has never been a stranger to tragedy, blood, and despair, but a place also that in its best moments has represented the most courageous, not to mention the most obstinate and colorful, strains in our history as a people. More specifically, he is from a terrain—Old Catawba!—that has given us Chapel Hill—and Thomas Wolfe, W. J. Cash, Jonathan Daniels, Frank Graham, and Terry Sanford, and head-for-head the best newspapers and some of the most civilized people in the United States, a state that deserves and receives the loyalty and memory of those who have been so nourished by the fineness of it. He knows the King James Bible; he knows the deepest laws and sanctions of this nation, and he is a practicing politician. He knows the full landscape of American sorrows, and he knows also, as all Southern boys and girls were brought up to know, just how thin is the skein of civility that holds America together.

Mr. Ehrlichman was preceded in the witness chair by the fraternity men and gentlemen athletes of Southern Cal. I doubt if they ever read Vann Woodward's *The Burden of Southern History* at the Pike House, or Mr. Faulkner's "The Bear," or Mr. Sandburg's *Lincoln,* and even had they been interested there were no writers in the vicinity they could call their own because it doesn't rain out there enough. In the most human contrast with Mr. Sam, they and their elders are bereft of a place, and of the past.

Then came their mentor, Mr. Ehrlichman. He spoke of "marching orders," "national security situations," and, again, "time frames"—crisp, cool, and arrogant, with lectures to Mr. Sam and his colleagues on the Fourth Amendment and executive prerogatives and the rampant evils of sex and drink among potential foes, never once so much as suggesting the smallest feeling for the delicacy and anguish and complexity of our nation.

For among the many dramas of this investigation, which is now becoming a monument to the best and the worst in us, with no middle ground here, one of the most basic of them is this contrast in cultures, in our very memory of ourselves: the old woebegone, whipped-down South, the South of our childhood, of Faulkner's summers of wisteria, of Mr. Sam's afternoons in court and getting his votes at the feed stores and seed stores and courthouse squares—and Mr. Ehrlichman's confection and cosmos of Southern California. Those like myself chose our side a long time ago.

Weep No More, My Lady

We called her "Mamie." For the last three years she had been in a nursing home in Yazoo City, Mississippi, my hometown, right around the corner from my mother's house. All day long, over and over, she would cry "Momma, Papa" and talk with people four generations gone. The last time I saw her, tiny and shriveled in her bed, completely blind and almost wholly deaf, out of her whirling shadows she took my hand and said, "Is that the boy? My boy always was a rascal." In her final lucid moment she whispered to my mother, "Put me in the ground next to Percy and close the gate behind you. I want to go home." She was weeping when she died.

She was ninety-seven, born the year the Yankee troops withdrew from Mississippi, the youngest of seventeen and the only one still alive. Her uncle was the first governor of Mississippi, even before it became a state; another uncle defeated Jefferson Davis for governor and was a U.S. Senator before the Civil War; her father was the best newspaper editor of his day there, and later served in the Confederacy as a major, taking to dirt-farming with one mule when Reconstruction came. Her mother, she told me as a boy, tended the wounded Yankee soldiers on the front porch after the Battle of Raymond. She was the repository of vanished times for me. Although she would not have understood had I told her, she helped me to have feeling for the few things that matter. I was nourished in the echoes of her laughter. She was my mainstay, my strength and salvation. She was my favorite human being.

When I was a boy, she and I took long walks around town in the gold summer dusk, out to the cemetery or miles and miles to the Old Ladies' Home, talking in torrents between the long silences. All about us were forests of crape myrtles and old houses faintly ruined. Widow ladies and spinsters sat on the galleries of the dark houses cooling themselves with paper fans, and we greeted each lady by turn, and then she told me who they were and what had happened to their people. We must have been an unlikely pair on those long-ago journeys, she in her flowing dress and straw hat, I barefoot in a T-shirt and blue jeans, with a sailor's cap on my head, separated by our sixty years. Only when I grew older did I comprehend that it was the years between us that made us close; ours was a symbiosis forged by time.

What are hills? How old are horses? Where do people go when they die? She always tried to answer me. But mostly she told me stories. Since she was the seventeenth child, she told me, her mother was so ashamed that she hid her as a baby under the blankets of the wagon when friends approached on the road. When the Methodist preacher came for fried chicken on Sundays, she always got a neck and a wing, because nothing else was left when the plate reached her end of the table. During a race riot after a political barbecue, five or six Negro men asked her to hide them, so she kept them in a deserted chickenhouse for two days and fetched them cornbread and buttermilk from the kitchen. One autumn twilight she took me to the old family home, sold to pay taxes long before, and under the house she sighted a beautiful white pebble, quite large, and she told me she had found it down by the town well when she was ten years old.

To my grandfather Percy, who made potato chips at the potato-chip factory, she was the sustenance of life; she was ever patient also with my two outrageous old-maid aunts, who in their blindness peregrinated about the house at all hours, carrying on conversations with garbage cans or brooms standing in corners or the hall furnace, waiting for the food to be served. One hot summer night many years ago, she went to get me a glass of water, and in the darkness broke her big toe on a rocker. To ease the pain until the doctor came, she smoked the only cigarette of her life, a rolled-up Bull Durham, saying to me, "I could get *addicted*." When I had my tonsils out in the hospital, I fought my way from under the ether, spitting blood on the bed, and then I saw her next to me, whispering, "My poor, poor boy." At nights, half asleep on the couch, drowsy in the cadences of the katydids, I absorbed in a reverie her aimless talk with her sisters—disasters of the flesh, people long forgotten, her Momma and Poppa—and heard the big clock on the mantel chime each quarter-hour.

She made her first trip to New York, to see me, when she was eighty-seven. It bemused her that the magazine I edited bore her family name, Harper, though she deemed it the Northern branch. She and my mother and I sat one evening at a sidewalk café in Greenwich Village; a number of racially mixed couples strolled past us, hand-in-hand. "I've never seen people carry on like that," my mother said. I attempted a reply. Then, quite gently, Mamie said, "It's a long way from home, son. *You* know that." Then she paused for a moment, looking across Sixth Avenue at nothing in particular, and added, "Maybe when we all get to heaven, *they'll* be white and *we'll* be black."

When the call came to me on Long Island that she had died, my son David and I rushed to LaGuardia and made the last flight back. It took us just eight hours to be in Yazoo, although we seemed in many ways to have traveled considerably farther than that.

Spring was on its way; the jonquils and burning bushes and Japanese magnolias were in bloom, and out in the delta the black land hummed with motion. But we were immersed in a web of death, for death in a small Southern town is like death in no other place. Everyone knows right away when someone has died, and there is a community apparatus to deal with the situation, old bonds of institutional grief almost primal in their unfolding. Having lived away so long, I had forgotten how they cope with it, death every day, death everlasting, among people who live in such proximity amid the familiar landmarks and places, punctuated only by the immemorial changes of the seasons.

But they do. They bring food and they talk among themselves about this death and others. They hover close in the web of death; they try hard to make mortality natural. Here in Yazoo, at the age of thirty-nine, I looked death in the face with stark comprehension for the first time.

In the funeral home she lay in the next room. I watched my son looking furtively from time to time in her direction. It was his first funeral. The sight of him there made me remember my first one, and looking at him now helped me know my son better. He is a Manhattan boy, and he lurked now in corners watching the whole town come through, my mother's church ladies, my father's fishing and domino friends. "He looks just like you did," they said. "He favors you." They admired his Yankee accent.

Later, when Mamie's funeral procession approached the church, turn-ing east at the courthouse, a black policeman stood in the center of the street at attention, holding his cap over his heart. We were to bury her in Raymond, fifty miles away, and now only five or six cars followed us, a meager parade, as we drove past the suburbs and shopping centers of old Mississippi, a lovely terrain of abrupt hills and kudzu vines being ripped away whole, and mammoth new expressways making something else entirely of the land she once knew.

We reached the old section of the Raymond cemetery before the hearse, and everyone got out to look around. Desolation awaited us. On this isolated and forlorn hill, the people who had settled her town were buried; all was moist now with decay, the broken, crumbled tombstones overgrown with weeds and Johnson grass. I walked with the preacher through the family plot, enclosed by its rusty iron fence, but the graves of all the Harpers had vanished. Only one remained: Samuel Dawson Harper, her eldest brother, born in 1851, died in 1905. Fifty yards away, down a rolling incline, was a larger fence enclosing fifty unidentified Confederate dead. I saw my son strolling among them, and among the older graves across the way, and a few moments later he walked up to me carrying a small broken tombstone, wordlessly laying it at my feet: "To Richard Edwards, 1828–1863, From His Friends the Confederate Soldiers." He was upset when I told him he could not take it back to New York.

"I hate to leave her in this awful place," my mother said; as she said it the hearse arrived. The men put the coffin and the flowers on the open grave, and we gathered about against the heavy wind and said "The Lord's Prayer." It was over in moments.

Yet people stayed, as if riveted to that place and time; they moved a distance from the grave to talk. I saw my son with the undertaker, watch-ing the coffin slowly descend into the ground. In the crowd a tall, angular man I did not know, a local man, caught me by the arm. "By God, you're Rae." Not Rae, I said. "Yes, by damn, you're *Rae*. You're the image of your father. You're Rae's boy."

I walked away from this strange lingering, and drifted alone up the hill. Wisps of clouds cast the terrain before me in gloom. Far below stretched the streets of the old town. The bell on the courthouse struck four, and, in a lane beyond, a child ran after a car tire that was rolling along. A dog barked in pursuit of the child; from near the grave there was laughter, and the minglings of a dozen voices.

In a rush I knew in my heart the sweetness and simplicity of her days on this earth. Alone on the hill, in a February wind, I grieved for Mamie.

It Took More Than Good Men
to Win the War

My old buddy James Dickey, poet, novelist, critic, actor, canoist, archer, guitar-picker, Clemson halfback when they used the single-wing, dipped into Washington from South Carolina the other day so the two of us could be with Maury Povich on the *Panorama* TV show, and we wandered around town the way we used to do on Manhattan Island when we were younger. He is on the cover of *Esquire* this month, in a life mask the drippings of which got into his eyes when the artist was working on him down in Boone, North Carolina, and he was blind for two days and had to be rushed to the doctors. This experience with blindness was the impulse behind the segment of his novel-in-progress in *Esquire* about fighter pilots in the Pacific in World War II, of which he was one, and it is a brilliant and haunted piece of work.

"I enjoyed laboring in these dark satanic mills," he says. "Is that Washington?" I asked. "No, that's Blake."

Big Jim, or sometimes just Jimbo to those of us who know he's a good man to ride the river with, was the Poet-in-Residence at the Library of Congress ten years ago. "I had a splendid office with the best view of the Capitol in the city. It's appropriate that the poet's office should have the finest view, don't you think?"

I don't know where that decade went, but I dropped in to see him one fine spring day in those surroundings and he took me to the window and said: "If that won't make an Amur-i-can out of us Southern boys, I don't know what will." Then he reached into his pocket and pulled out a key, unlocked a bulky door off to the side, and led me into a chamber filled with old volumes. He took down one of them and handed it to me, and I began reading a journal of someone in longhand. "You know who you're reading? You're reading my man—Mr. Shelley." And we pored over it shyly, like miscreants, the way we used to sit on our haunches and read comic books in the drug store without having to buy them.

Later on that afternoon in 1966, we went on over to the bar of the Democratic Club in the Congressional Hotel, watching the politicians steal their 3 p.m. nip and relax with favored secretaries, where Big Jim told me he was on the committee at the Library which had just offered $60,000 for the voluminous correspondence between T. S. Eliot and Groucho Marx. Eliot had initiated the exchange, because he wanted to elicit Groucho's views on entertainment, "and Groucho by no means came off worse," he said.

After a while we got into conversation with a very junior congressman from New York, an arrogant fellow, in which Dickey told him there were moments here and there, such as this one, when he wished Jubal Early's raid on Washington in '64 had ended more happily. Our poet laureate convinced the congressman that he was a salesman for Dickey Business Machines in Atlanta, and ended up selling him some kind of miniature computer for $350, promising to bill him after delivery.

That was the day I believe I gave him the idea for one of his best poems, when I told him about the time the Yazoo High Indians went up into the delta to play Belzoni in basketball, the toughest group of hard-noses in all of cotton country, where we suffered broken bones and bruises and the worst abuses from the drunken partisans in the gallery and still won by one point on my jump-shot with nineteen seconds to go, and Muttonhead Shepherd from the back of the bus heading back to Yazoo in that sea of dead cotton stalks shouted: "We got the bastards, boys, away from home with nineteen seconds left!"

The line from his poem reads: "Boys, we won! We won away from home in the last minute!"

That was the day, too, that Big Jim told me he was starting a novel about "plain old fear, old horrible fear," set around a canoe trip four Atlanta boys took down a spectral river in north Georgia, and this, of course, became *Deliverance*.

I've never known a writer around whom the stories cluster so vividly. This is because he believes that friendship among other things is a brotherhood of entertainment, and because he is much beloved. One afternoon of high winds and fog, we met in the bar of the St. Moritz in New York.

We were going to do a tape of a national television show (as it turned out, he got extremely angry because we were preceded by a smart-dog act), and we sat in the bar drinking sourmash and quoting poetry to each other, and as the day waxed Big Jim quoted from his work in a voice which seemed to carry a long way. The maitre d' came over to our table and said, "We want you gentlemen out of here."

"I beg your pardon, kind sir?"

"We want you to leave."

His expression was incredulous, and he wrinkled his brows and said, in a Brando whisper: "Do you realize who you're kicking out of this bar? America's greatest poet and his friend, the editor-in-chief of *Harper's Magazine*."

The maitre d' said, "Out!"

We got in a cab to head uptown, morosely watching the steam bellow out of the sewers, and the cab-driver, having heard our Southern accents, said: "You gentlemen aren't from around here, are you?"

We said no. Then he proceeded to launch into a tirade against our black brethren, and a vicious thing it was, the likes of which I never heard in the Mississippi delta.

We were separated from the driver by a wall of bullet-proof glass, and Dickey leaned down, hands cupped over his mouth, and said through the aperture where you put the money: "Mr. Liebowitz, if there's anything I can't stand it's an amateur bigot."

"Beg pardon?"

"We had the finest fighting men in the field in the history of warfare. Only our machines failed us. We had only one ball-bearings factory in the whole Confederacy, in Richmond, Virginia. We were so desperate in 1865 that we produced only 423 ball-bearings—423 dead Liebowitzes."

Liebowitz was baffled—eyes widening—and maybe even a little fearful. After a silence, he ventured: "What are you gentlemen doing up here now?"

"We come up to buy a ball-bearings factory," Big Jim said.

We were having dinner the other night in a place called Tiberio on K Street with his wife Maxine and his son Chris, who works for the book-section of the *Post,* and Chris's wife and son, a playful boy who calls his grandfather "Funny Man." Big Jim talked a little about Washington.

"Well, it's like Atlanta, or maybe Atlanta's like it. When I came to the Library of Congress, we talked to the people about housing. They said the easiest thing to do was go to Maryland. Only a few go to Virginia, they said. It's a long drive. I said, Maxine, don't pay any attention to these people who talk about convenience. You go over and look for a house in Virginia, because I want to live in the South.

"When I first came into the poetry chair—it's kind of equivalent to the Poet Laureate of England, you know—I was bewildered by the different kinds of opportunities of the most unusual sort in this town. My Lord, a man can drink himself to death on the cocktail circuit."

But he was impressed by the Library in the American cultural scene, how they bring in fine writers, for instance, and give them good audiences, and the video-tape projects, so that a hundred years from now students of our literature can see William Styron and John Updike among others, conversing about writing.

"I was dismayed by what I saw of the political back-biting. But I liked a great number of the politicians. Mark Hatfield. He was such a straightforward fellow, very well informed, the kind of person the American political system should be proud of. Gene McCarthy. I like him first of all because he's a poet, a great friend of the arts as Kennedy was, but I suspect Kennedy had nothing of the insights into the creative imagination that McCarthy does. Gene took such a brave stand against the buffalo stampede of Johnson's forces, and he beat 'em. He's going to give it one more try, probably the last. It'll have something of an impact, and that's enough, that's worth it.

"But in Washington, despite not wanting to venture out into the streets, you genuinely do feel you're at the hub of where history is being made, where truly important things are happening all the time. You don't get that in Ellijay, Georgia. Add to that the personal gossip about political figures, and your eyes swim like gyroscopes. And all this varies and shifts, this tremendous excitement from day to day.

"When one lives in Washington with an attitude that's the most constructive, one feels the way Mencken did, that the American political scene is essentially a circus, so just sit back and enjoy it."

We went on down the next day to be on *Panorama*. Big Jim in a widebrimmed hat with a flask of Jack Daniels concealed in a pocket.

My old friend has been known to galvanize a setting, like the perambu-lating poets of old who were also performers, and the big cavernous studio on Wisconsin Avenue seemed to whip into life all of a sudden. He came on with Maury Povich and read from a long new poem of his called "The Zodiac" about a man obsessed with the galaxies, and talked about literature, and about movies and the other forms.

"I believe in the word. I'll always fall back on the word." He told about his cousin Bill Dickey down in Georgia. "He was not just a drunk, he was the drunk. Alcoholics Anonymous sent two fellows out under the buddy-system to try to help my cousin Bill, and they lost two of their best men."

Big Jim showed himself in these moments under the klieg lights, all the human qualities, all his vulnerabilities and his strengths. I've known Maury Povich for several years, and liked him, and have seen him im-prove to the point that he's one of the best interviewers in the trade, and Maury later said that, out of the whole steady stream of Washington people and visiting celebrities, "this was the most meaningful interview I ever had."

Then it was Big Jim and me talking, as we always did years ago in the saloons along the East Side when we were twelve years younger and it was good to talk about writing with an editor or two always there to listen, and about the seed stores, feed stores, and courthouse squares of vanished days, and when you would stand on the balconies of tall build-ings with beautiful hostesses around and shake your glasses as Thomas Wolfe liked to do and hear the tinkle of the ice and watch the lights of the great city come on.

Later, standing outside in the cold sunshine on Wisconsin Avenue with some lovely television ladies, one last nip at the flask and Big Jim was gone, dashing to a taxi to meet Gene McCarthy.

The cab turned, and from the window an exultant shout in my direc-tion: "Boys, we won! We won away from home in the last minute!"

Of Northern Fears, Southern Realities, and Jimmy Carter

BRIDGEHAMPTON, N.Y.—Why the lingering antipathy toward him here in the East? Is it the fear that he equivocates on the big issues—that there is little difference between him and Ford or Reagan, as some liberals have actually suggested? Or that they will be singing "Bringing in the Sheaves" in the Northern parochial schools and that Jewish boys henceforth will be baptized by full immersion of the head at bar mitzvahs? Or that America will become ethnically pure again? Or that a "twice-born" Christian will deny the state of Israel's sovereignty? Or is there something a little more complicated at work here?

"The Carters are clearly nice people," Harriet Van Horne writes. "But in my Yankee Presbyterian soul, I'm uncomfortable with them." A rabbi on Long Island remarked the other day, "Northern Jews on the whole are suspicious of Southerners." An architect from out here said to me: "It's the old fear of latent Southern fascism. I can't conceive of a Southerner, especially one with such fundamentalist beliefs, putting the welfare of the country before his background and his religion." Recently a friend from New York said, "If Carter's elected, I'm afraid he'll make Washington into a Southern town."

But it's already a Southern town, I said. It was a Southern town from the minute they lifted it out of the swamps.

"I didn't mean that," he replied. "I'm afraid he'll just turn the whole Government over to Southerners. And I'm not alone."

In her book *Lyndon Johnson and the American Dream*, Doris Kearns quotes L. B. J.:

"The burden of national unity rests heaviest on one man, the President. And I did not believe, any more than I ever had, that the nation would unite indefinitely behind any Southerner. . . . My experience in office had confirmed this reaction. I was not thinking just of the derisive articles about my style, my clothes, my manner, my accent, and my family. I was thinking of a more deep-seated and far-reaching attitude—a disdain for the South that seems to be woven into the fabric of national experience . . . an automatic reflex, unconscious or deliberate. . . ."

It was personal insecurity more than political analysis which evoked Johnson's assessment, as Miss Kearns suggests, and I do not for a moment believe Carter suffers the demons of paranoia as L. B. J. did. If anything, rather the contrary. But there is a seed of truth in Johnson's words about this disdain in the fabric of our experience, as any white Southerner who has dwelled in the North will testify.

Right now this disaffection has become a national issue—I can sense it everywhere, stirring on the surfaces as it never really did in the primaries—just as much as John Kennedy's Catholicism was a critical concern prior to his historic declaration to the Baptist ministers (in whose company I was sitting as a disguised evangelic in the Crystal Ballroom of the Rice Hotel in Houston that September night in 1960) that his religion would not interfere with the Presidency.

Personally, I suspect this Northern disaffection would be only slightly less pervasive if Carter were a High Anglican with a less-pragmatic and more directly ideological set of views and had made succinct pronouncements on every question from the financial crisis of the five boroughs to the Supreme Court decision on sodomy. What does matter in the present circumstances is that the United States has never had a President from the Deep South.

These fears that abound are misguided, certainly, responsive as they are to the regional clichés and the negative images, and damnably naïve about a lot of things, including the realities of national politics as well as the high political genius of a man who came from nowhere to secure what will certainly be a first-ballot nomination after five months of arduous primaries. Reminiscent, too, of the thinking of those Eastern liberals who chose not to vote for Hubert Humphrey in 1968 because they wanted to "punish" him—and after one of the closest elections in our history we finally know what we got *that* time.

But these are well-meaning people, more or less typical of that sizable Northern community with practically no knowledge of, much less direct experience with, the complexity and pluralism of the South, of the nobilities which have existed there, or of that strain in its uncommon past which has endowed it with an enlightened humanitarian legacy.

I believe it to Carter's advantage, and to the country's, that he sooner or later address himself forthrightly to these fears, just as Kennedy did before his detractors in Houston. It would lend affirmation to the belief in many Northern circles that it is a profoundly encouraging development for the whole nation that the Deep South has finally produced a leader that the rest of America might accept.

It would rank in importance with that classic confrontation in recent American politics—the one between Senator Ervin of the Carolina foothills and John Erlichman, when Mr. Sam afforded the country a human insight into the difference between the roots of his heritage and its faith in constitutional governance, and the cosmos and confection of Nixon's America.

And the spirit and experience behind such an unabashed and much-needed testimonial could only buttress what some now perceive: that the very presence of a Carter on the national scene has already begun to heal those old enduring dislocations and apprehensions which have existed between North and South since the earliest days of the Republic.

Mr. Carter would never say it this way, of course, but these are a handful of the ironies which, at the risk of incurring a little healthy anger, I consider relevant:

Intelligent Southerners have made a more conscientious effort to understand the non-Southern regions of this country, the disparities in them, the dispositions and impulses of their history, than their Northern counterparts have made to understand the South. There has been a reluctance on the part of many Northerners to comprehend the complexities of Southern history, the burdens of its past, and the manifestations of its better nature.

The watershed of our experience as a nation was the Civil War, the death and rebirth of a civilization, and on this I find most Northerners uninformed, not of the names and dates and generals and battles, but of the human forces behind that cleavage, the anguish and tragedy of it, the things it solved and the things it failed to solve, and what it was beyond the bloodshed of a million American boys which eventually brought us together again.

I think it meaningful that most intelligent Southerners have an abiding feeling for Lincoln, for all he represented; perhaps because of its time of deprivation (and no province of America has ever suffered more destruction than Mr. Carter's Georgia) there has always been an underlying mood in the South which took to its heart Lincoln's favorite epitaph:

> *Here lies poor Johnny Kongapod;*
> *Have mercy on him, Gracious God,*
> *As he would do if he was God,*
> *And You were Johnny Kongapod.*

Most Northerners still view the South as a segregated society, ignoring the fact that a combination of the Federal presence and its own best instincts have transformed it in the last fifteen years into the most racially integrated region in America, as if between the whites and blacks of the South—the oldest and most indigenous of all the American hyphenates, in the historian C. Vann Woodward's phrase—we have witnessed in our lifetime the first ritualization of a common-law marriage.

It was, in fact, the political emergence of the blacks in the South, and more specifically in Georgia during his years as Governor, which allowed Jimmy Carter to challenge George Wallace on his home ground and to launch a serious national campaign, for without their support he would have been doomed from the beginning.

Inherent in all this, many Northerners, too, have persisted in looking at the South as a monolith, without much diversity or nuance, blurring the differences among states, among individuals, among social values and political movements. Many do not begin to acknowledge the liberalism, often with its populist overtones, which has undergirded much of the South for generations, or those Southerners, often at physical hazard, who have stood for something opposite to the Bilbos, the Faubuses, and the Wallaces.

More specifically, they know little of the humanitarian impulse which has emerged among the Southern Baptists in the last generation, a new strain in Carter's church which upholds pluralism and social reform as necessary to the greater good. And many have forgotten, as Rabbi Marc Tannenbaum has reminded us, that the traditions of religious liberty in American began, after all, with Roger Williams, a Baptist.

Mr. Carter is heir to all this. Far from being an incubus he has had to spurn, or to escape, these things in his heritage as a Southerner have constituted a pillar, a prop, for his national view and his civilized convictions. They will strengthen him in his unmistakable desire to campaign in the most progressive traditions of the party and, barring the unforeseen, after he is elected President as he is surely going to be, to govern in the enduring interests of the nation.

My Friend Marcus Dupree

Marcus Dupree is 6 feet 3 and weighs a little more than 230 pounds. He has been timed in the 100-yard dash in 9.8 seconds. It is almost godlike, one might say, for a football player that large to run that fast. Indeed, there is little question that in the South football is a religion.

I first got to know Marcus when he was seventeen years old, a senior in the high school at Philadephia, Mississippi, in Neshoba County. That was more than two years ago, and even then he was a legendary figure in his native state and in much of Dixie. He came from a poor black family; he lived with his mother, who was a schoolteacher, his crippled brother, Reggie, and his grandparents.

At the time, Marcus was the most acclaimed and sought-after high school football player in America—a swift and powerful running back whom many were already beginning to compare with the heroic Herschel Walker of Georgia. As a writer who had just returned after many years in the North to live again in my home state, I found myself ineluctably drawn to the accomplishments and talent of the young man, not to mention the tortured place that had produced him.

He went out into the world a year ago September shouldering a great burden of dreams and aspirations—not only his own but also those of his townspeople and even, to some extent, an entire region. A question remained to be answered: How good was he, really? What was he made of?

The locale of Marcus's past and his people was suffused with its remembrance of self-destruction. In the civil rights struggles of the 1960s, Neshoba County was a symbol of recalcitrance and brutality. Two young Northern Jews, Michael Schwerner and Andrew Goodman, and a Mississippi black, James Earl Chaney, were murdered there with the connivance of the police. They had been organizing blacks to register to vote. Their disappearance—along with the harassments, beatings, burnings, and mob cruelties—attracted the attention of the world. "This is a terrible town, the worst I've seen," Martin Luther King Jr. said. "There is a complete reign of terror here."

The lifetime of Marcus Dupree paralleled the town's agonized evolution from Klan terror to civility and decency. He was born one month before the murders. He was a member of the Mount Nebo Missionary Baptist Church, which had opened its doors to the civil rights workers and where a memorial had been erected to the three slain men. His high school graduating class in 1982 would be the first in which whites and blacks had gone through all twelve grades together.

Marcus was a shy, ingratiating youngster who wore eyeglasses. During football games, he wore over his copious Afro a red hairnet that his mother had sewed for him. I grew to sense a complexity in him which he had not yet faced and a sly humor among those he trusted that was fine as rain. His brother, Reggie, then nine years old, had cerebral palsy and walked with crutches. One day at the high school, as Reggie hesitated before some steps, I saw Marcus bodily lift him over them, then gently put him down. Later that year, Marcus said something that stunned me with its simplicity: "I guess I run for both of us."

From the very start, I was touched by Marcus's struggle to live up to his extraordinary talent. On the poor little football fields of east central Mississippi, I saw him score long touchdowns I could not believe. There was magic in the way he ran. Drama enveloped him; inevitably, later, envy and controversy would also. He scored fourteen touchdowns in his last three games, including five in the final one, to break Herschel Walker's schoolboy record of eighty-six touchdowns.

He was a good student and a favorite among his teachers. His coach, Joe Wood, a thirty-eight-year-old white man, said: "You get to know somebody coachin' him three years. Some people are good human beings and not good athletes. Some are good athletes and not good human beings. Marcus is both." White and black, the younger boys of Philadelphia emulated the way he walked. A black factory worker said: "He's a gift from God, a gift to us. He's bringing this town together." The mayor said: "I'm downright thankful for him."

It struck me that a considerable burden was being placed on a small-town black boy who had barely turned seventeen. These were circumstances of immense irony, ambiguity, and complexity, for this burden involved whites, blacks, a new and fragile kind of unity—a symbol of the South itself.

Every major football power in the country sought to recruit him. "If I can do well in college ball," Marcus said, "I'll be able to help my family. I just want to go to a good school, and I want to play. My dream is to finish college and to make the pros."

As I followed him through his senior year, I decided I would write a book about him. I eventually discovered this to be a tale about two small-town Mississippians—a seventeen-year-old black and a middle-aged white—and the way they responded to each of their generations and to their common bewitched ground.

As he would do, I too at his age had left my town in Mississippi, everything I ever knew and cared for and honored, for a strange, teeming university. The young black's odyssey into the greater world would nearly coincide with the middle-aged white's return from a long exile. And perhaps there was an ironic logic in something deeper—that while the white man's progenitors were founding Mississippi as statesmen and warriors, the young black's forebears were crossing in boats from Africa and toiling in cotton under the sun. He and I sprang from a different yet mutual heritage.

Marcus narrowed his final choices to six colleges. He made trips to the campuses, including UCLA, where he was introduced to Beverly Hills, Malibu, and the golden girls of the television age. He also visited the University of Pittsburgh, after which he told his teachers: "It was so cold, my hair froze."

Shortly before his "national signing date," the town gave him an Appreciation Day, where several hundred townspeople paid him tribute. "This couldn't have happened fifteen years ago," the editor of *The Neshoba Democrat* said.

Four days later, he signed to attend the University of Oklahoma. Its team was on national television often, he said, and he would have a shot there at the Heisman Trophy.

Before he left, I had a long talk with him in the bleachers of the deserted football field. "I wish I could stay in Mississippi," he said. "I'd love to stay in Mississippi. Sometimes you just have to give up the finer things in life to get what you want."

Marcus left for his freshman year at Oklahoma as one of most heralded high school athletes in the country. Had it all been too much too soon?

He soon answered the question. He became the first freshman ever to lead Oklahoma in rushing. He scored 13 touchdowns and gained 1144 yards on 146 carries, for an average of almost 8 yards a carry. In the Fiesta Bowl, he gained 239 yards against the No. 1 defensive team in the nation in only half a game, playing with bruised ribs, a broken finger, and a sore hamstring. *Football News* selected him Freshman of the Year.

As his sophomore year was about to begin, he was being mentioned as a leading candidate for the Heisman Trophy, but then the pressures intensified. His hamstring injury had caused him to miss spring football, and he hurt an ankle early in the season. A cover story in *Sports Illustrated* in the summer had portrayed him as a lazy, overweight prima donna who barely got along with his coach, Barry Switzer. It was suggested he might leave for the pros next year.

The description of him in the article certainly did not sound like the Marcus I knew. Some sportwriters came to his defense. The papers in Jackson, Mississippi, cited his summer work with white and black children and his self-discipline as an athlete. I saw him before the season began, and I was proud of how articulate and self-possessed he had become. He was looking forward to getting back to school and working hard. He spoke well of his coach and said he hoped the team might win the national championship. I saw no sign of a swollen ego.

As the season opened, he gained 138 yards as Oklahoma defeated Stanford 27–14. In the next game, against Ohio State, he hurt his knee after gaining 30 yards as Oklahoma lost 24–14. He missed the third game, a win over Tulsa, but came back in the fourth to rush for 151 yards and three touchdowns.

The challenge to him now, at age nineteen, is more acute than ever. Yet I have never for a moment lost faith in Marcus, nor, I sense, has he in himself. "Pressure is only what you make it," he said a long time ago, long before he performed before crowds of 75,000 and on national television. Or, as a young hometown white who knew him well observed: "There's something about growing up in Philadelphia, Mississippi— white or black. When things get difficult and there's more on the line, you don't quit. You get mean. He ain't worried. He's thinkin' right now about goin' on that field and *doin' good*."

I sense that Marcus has not faced the half of it yet, the pain and discouragement. And someday—I hope only in the distant future—his skills will fail him. Perhaps the way he copes with that will prove the final measure, not of the boy, but of the man.

What It Takes for a Son to Understand a Father

He died twenty-six years ago this week, in our small town in Mississippi. I was twenty-four and on my honeymoon in Texas when I got word he only had a few more hours. I rushed out on the first plane, but by the time I got there he was gone. Across the dim, distant frontiers of death I ask myself now: Who was he? What was he like? And who indeed was I?

I am a father too now, and I comprehend more than I once did the lines of Dr. Gibbs in Wilder's *Our Town:* "I tell you, Mrs. G., there's nothing so terrifying in the world as a son. The relation of father to a son is the damnedest, awkwardest——." Surely it is one of the most fundamental of human relationships, deep in the blood and primitive in its intensity, baffling in its emotions and ambivalences, in the pain and joy on both sides.

I grew up in an environment I could understand, one familiar and accessible to me. I knew the people of the town. My father knew and was known by them and, as in such locales of that nearly vanished day, my father's friends knew me and helped me. As with all sons of all epochs, I surmise now, I had problems in being merely "Rae Morris's boy."

The father-figure remains essential to our society, and the *absence* of it is so often destructive. I have known fathers who consciously chose to neglect their sons, who wittingly or unwittingly crossed that tortured divide beyond forgiveness or redemption, or who were cruel to their sons or sought to make them into their own image. I have known fathers, too, who would give them the final measure of the heart's devotion. Although this was never remotely spoken between us, and never could have been, I understand in the hard perspective of the years that my father was always there when I needed him.

I was not merely an only son, but an only child. From the mists of remembrance I see how tall and gaunt he was. He was from the hills of western Tennessee, and he had come to the Deep South, of all places and at all times, during the Great Depression. His mother died when he was small, and he grew up with aunts and cousins; he was only able to finish high school. He was a hunter and a fisherman, an indomitable country athlete and baseball player whose nickname was "Hooks" for the way he could hook-slide. Late into life, they still called him "Hooks" in Tennessee and recalled his willowy grace. His own father, from whom I got my name, had served in the Tennessee House of Representatives with Cordell Hull. When my father was eighteen, he enlisted in the Army for World War I and was waiting with the other Tennessee boys in New York for a troop ship to Europe when the Armistice came. I am unable to imagine him as a teenager wandering the streets of Manhattan.

It never occurred to me to question the dislocations he must have suffered marrying into a volatile, proper Mississippi family rooted in its lost, dispossessed past. I doubt if he gave much thought to the Confederacy, or the aristocratic South of my maternal forebears. Once, as we sat at the halftime of a college football game and the Ole Miss marching band came out with a Rebel flag half the size of the football field, he said to me: "Don't they know that damned war is over?"

He was *country,* in the way that he was tuned to its rhythms and its cycles, while my mother's people were garrulous, changeable, touched with charisma and given to histrionic flourishes, all this suffused with the tenacious, indwelling past. My mother was a pianist, an organist, a teacher, a graduate of Millsaps and of a Chicago conservatory, a preeminent *talker;* he spoke only when he deemed it necessary. Did he sometimes wonder what he had gotten himself into? Did he miss his hills of home and the majestic Tennessee River?

He ran a service station, distributed gasoline, was a bookkeeper. With scant success he helped me with my arithmetic; in high school, when I got to algebra, he said: "Maybe you're a writer." He read *True Detective* and *Field & Stream* and never went to the movies. He attended the American Legion meetings and entered the First Methodist Church once a year, at Easter, and sat in the back pew for a swift getaway. Whenever he sighted the preacher coming into our house to pray, he retreated to the backyard and hid in the Johnson grass, and I would go out there after a while and he would ask, "Is he gone yet?"

The swamp bottom of the delta woods was a more civilized place for him than the Rotary Club; Wolf Lake when the white perch were biting surpassed any cocktail party, and the firemen, mechanics, bootleggers, and rural World War I men who were not allowed into the country club—they preferred poker and dominoes at Firehouse No. 2—were likelier company than most of the respectable bourgeoisie. He was a "liberal," I sense now, in that time and place, although I suspect he did not know the word.

"If they pay taxes, they should vote," he once said to me of the Negroes, and then in a most uncharacteristic tirade he told me of the rich white men who took up the church collection plates on Sunday and cheated the blacks the rest of the week. He was close to a black dentist, and a Jew who became the mayor was one of his best friends.

In that age before television and shopping centers and suburbias, he taught me to love the quiet, unsettled places; we trekked the great woods where water sprang up in every spongy footprint. He taught me also to love dogs and baseball. Almost every summer afternoon when the heat was not unbearable, we would go out to the old baseball field to hit flies. I would stand in center field, and he would station himself with a fungo at home plate. Old Skip, the most honored of my boyhood dogs, would get in the outfield with me and retrieve the modest dribblers or the ones that went too far. Then, after an hour or more of this, my father would shout, "I'm whupped!" and we would quit for a while. To this day I could show you the precise intersection on Monroe Street where I asked him as we rode in the big green De Soto with Old Skip in back: If a batter hits a triple, does that count on his batting average as three hits? "Of course not," he replied. Years later, when I was in school in Oxford, England, he telephoned me from across the Atlantic to tell me Old Skip had died. Across that great distance he said: "I'm mighty sad."

My mother relentlessly criticized him in their many contretemps: Why did he never put on a coat and tie or go to the socials or to the men's Bible class the way the other men did? The only time he ever laid a hand on me was after I threw a glass of buttermilk on my mother for trying to comb my hair for me—a backhand across the posterior, but I could tell his heart was not in it. When, at age nine, I refused to take any more six-a-week piano lessons from her on the Steinway baby grand in the front room, she grew intemperate. "Let him alone to grow," he said to her. On early mornings before school as I lay in my bed next to Old Skip, I could drowsily hear him in the next room talking to her about me.

What, I wonder, did all this signify to me then? Why does the meaning of things, like rivulets in the springtime streams, pass one by at that age? Ours was a nonverbal relation: we never talked about anything "important." Perhaps there are some things, I see now, that people with an emotional involvement cannot tell one another; I see that there are things too delicate to be talked about in such a relation and that it is best not even to try. Yet what lay beneath the shadow and the act? Could I have fathomed then his regard for the unprivileged underdog, or that baseball might be an expression of love?

And what, pray, did I make then of the long pilgrimage he made for me? As I grew older I often pondered that question. One day, just before I was to graduate from high school, he turned from the newspaper and told me, quite simply, that I should leave Mississippi. There was a lack of *opportunity* here, he said, but was he thinking too of *doom?* Of the need to move away from first recognitions? Shortly after that he departed alone on the bus for Austin, six hundred miles away, to investigate the campus of what he had sometimes heard was the best and certainly the biggest state university in the South, the University of Texas. He returned a week later. "That's one hell of a place they got out there," he said to me. They had a main building twenty-eight stories high, he said, a baseball field dug right out of stone, artificial moonlight for street lamps, and the finest student newspaper in the United States. "I think you should go to school out there," he said. "There's nothin' in this state to match it."

To assert his God-given independence, I recognize now, a son must in the nature of us move away from his father. My own father must have sensed this when he went out to Texas for me those years ago. Surely he must have feared for me, a provincial hometown boy leaving all the settled qualities I knew on such a lonely odyssey, just as he must have known he would miss me. It was part of his legacy to me.

He wrote me letters every two weeks on an old Remington when I was in college, mainly about sports. When a member of the board of regents of the University of Texas criticized me for irresponsibility as editor of the student daily, he wrote this personage an eight-page letter defending me, to which the eminent Lone Star oilman deigned not to reply; I only came across a copy of the letter years later, hidden in the drawer of a dresser. Once, on a visit home from college, he told me he had just read a novel—*Something of Value*, I recall, by Robert Ruark. Did he understand I was learning to care for literature, and was he trying to share something with me? In the age-old snobbism of growing up, I spurned his solicitude.

"I can give good advice on how to raise someone else's son," a friend of mine said to me. "But when it comes to my own, the emotion and affection choke me up, make me speechless. It's a hell of a lot harder being a father than I ever thought it was when I was a son."

These are elemental instincts, biblical in the unfolding. Can any boy become his own man until his father dies, literally or symbolically? It is good that sons outlast fathers.

I have another memory, of going with a comrade now living in New England to a nursing home in his native South to bring back his aged father to live with his family. The pristine joy on the old man's face when the son came into his room to take him home, their affectionate embrace, were to me an imperishable affirmation.

It has taken me a long time to get to know him. But much in life comes full circle sooner or later, and I discover myself dreaming about him these days—his loping gait in the delta woods with the shotgun over his shoulder, his quiet drawl, the way he chuckled deep in his throat.

There was an ineffable moment for me not too long ago, a sudden stunning recognition. I was with my own son, who saw someone he knew and stood to greet him. He tilted his head slightly, moved shyly backward a step or two, smiled, extended his hand in a downward flourish. In that transitory instant I saw the precise image of my father, the same gesture I remembered of him in minute exactitude, and in shadowy profile across old time I saw him there again from my boyhood, the stark physical similarity leaping out at me without warning or even premonition, and I heard an inner voice whispering to me: *"There he is."*

The years are passing, and they remind me anew that we are born alone and we die alone. But along the way, as we traverse the days, the relationship of father and son, so strange and incalculable, can assuage the journey.

The last time I saw him, as he lay in the hospital dying, I sat next to his bed, talking with him about baseball. The preacher came in, and the two of them recited the Lord's Prayer. When the preacher left, I tried to work up my nerve to say, "If I ever have a boy, I'll name him after you." I could not say it. But when I stood to leave—to go to Texas to get married—he turned his head away from me and said, sitting hunched-up on the edge of the bed, "No matter what happens, boy, I'll always be watchin' out for you."

Capote Remembered

Truman was my neighbor on eastern Long Island for many years. It was a placid neighborhood of old villages and frosty inlets and ponds full of wild duck and Canada geese and flat, verdant potato fields which swept to the sand dunes and the ocean—a settled place touched with the past. He had a secluded house, hidden behind tall hedges, not far from the Atlantic in Wainscott. He was so often alone.

I lived on Church Lane in Bridgehampton, only two or three miles away. It was the 1970s and I had left New York City. You will often find Southerners in faraway Northern places like Bridgehampton, especially the artists, and their tendency is often to congregate, out of old shared instincts. Usually it is not that they have turned their backs on their native region—far from it. But where does memory best flourish? The imagination? The sharp, sequestered beauty of the great Eastern littoral provides for some the release and detachment so often elusive back home. It is perhaps a matter of personal choice, and of psychic balance.

I had a wonderful black Lab named Pete. Pete and I are strolling up the sidewalk on the main street of Bridgehampton. An enormous Buick with a small man, so small that his nose barely rises above the dashboard, as in the "Kilroy Was Here" drawings of World War II, stops before us.

"Willie! Pete! Hop in and let's ride around and *gossip*."

Pete gets in back, I in front. "Boys, I can't wait to tell you about my conversation at lunch in Le Côte Basque with Princess Radziwill yesterday." He gestures dramatically and pays little attention to the road.

We are around the block and toward the ocean. Finally we are travelling in long widening circles around the dunes and potato fields. Truman is telling us of his social life in Manhattan, a brilliant, perfervid monologue touched with flamboyant dervishes and irreverent pirouettes. Now he is talking of Bennett and Phyllis Cerf—some party for a U.S. Senator—and Babe Paley in the Four Seasons, and a tryst in a New Jersey motel between a WASP female socialite and a mobster. And a lunch in the Plaza, I think with Kay Graham. In the back seat Pete is scratching a flea: Truman is talking about the Princess again.

"How old were you when you wrote *Other Voices, Other Rooms?*" I interrupt.

He pauses over the dashboard. "So very young," he says. "Oh so very young and brilliant."

He negotiates the turn at Church Lane. He tells me of his latest recipe for quiche. "Oh, Willie," he says. "How naive you are! Your simplicity! The things I could tell you!"

Nearly four years after his death in the cool confines of Joanne Carson's house in Beverly Hills, Truman was back in the news. In May 1988, Simon and Schuster brought out a major Capote biography by Gerald Clarke, a biography that followed on the heels of publication of *The Truman Capote Reader* and *Answered Prayers*—or at least the bits and pieces of *Answered Prayers* that the scholars and the literary grave diggers have been able to find. Truman would have been amused by it all. He always did understand the spotlight, perhaps better than the rest of us. *Answered Prayers* was to have been Truman's great novel, and the promise of it kept attention focused on him even in those later years when he was known by many people more for the words that came out of his mouth than the words that ended up on the printed page.

There were many words that came out of that mouth, of course. From the articles that have appeared since Truman's death, I suppose it is obvious that in his last days he was beclouded by drugs and booze. The declining days of fine writers—especially, I think, in America—bring on the interviewers; these last days are painful and lonely, and they are too often the days that are remembered. I suspect that the trauma of writing *In Cold Blood*—those long years spent in the company of killers—was what led Truman to drugs and eventually damaged the soul of the boy who wrote *A Christmas Memory*. But for all the sad glimpses of him in his latter, suffering days that the books and the biographies and the excerpts give us, I prefer to remember another Truman, one I shared food and time and talk with on the shores of the island. This is the same

Truman I still meet when I pull his books from my shelves. This is, I like to believe, the true Truman, the one that refuses to be obscured by gossip—even his own.

I liked Truman, and, for whatever reason, he liked me. I don't know if this mutual affection was because we were both small town Southerners in a place where there were few of us to be found. It may well be so; the small town South never left Truman, though it always seemed subtly at war with his cosmopolitan instincts. When I first got to know him, I suspected he had given too much of his heart's core to those cosmopolitan instincts, to a style of living and a company of companions about whom he cared too much, a company that chose to turn upon him in his twilight time.

Truman may well not have agreed. Though he was very small, and he had that high, shrill, lispy voice, touched by the South, that was as distinctive a voice as I ever heard (there is no way to mimic the way he talked, although even those of us who cared for him tried when he was not around), he claimed he was impervious to bullying. The other children never bullied him when he was growing up, he said, because he had the most wicked tongue in town; the adults he later seemed a child among likely never bullied him for the same reason.

Truman's voice came from his past as a solitary orphan brought up by old maid Alabama cousins, from his life as the kid who started writing and getting drunk on wine at age twelve. The immemorial Christmas morning in Alabama was an indelible part of him—as was the dual hanging in the state prison in Kansas he captured in *In Cold Blood*. These were the two poles of Truman's art—observing himself and observing others.

I cannot help but believe that both poles had much to do with his raising in the ornately polite society that was so often found in the old small town South, a society that rewarded you well for keen observation and encouraged a child to listen. Truman did listen. He could hear what people said, and what they meant, and then get that on paper in a clear and clean way that escapes most writers. Other writers could not help but envy Truman that which, if he had been a singer, might have been called his purity of tone.

But that purity may well have been a curse as well as a charm. When

I grew to know Truman on Long Island, Southern boys sharing a familiarity of knowledge, I wondered if perhaps the keenness of his observation had begun to wear on him. What he could put on paper was never quite as true as what he could see, and so there were long periods in which he published little, and the constant unmet promise of *Answered Prayers*. Truman could talk what he saw, could keep the audience at bay with the wicked intelligence of his tongue, but though he may have archly realized that all literature is gossip, he knew as well that all gossip is not literature. As he got older, he found it harder to write, he said, because his standards were too high. It was easier when he was twenty-five, but at fifty he expected too much of himself. For all his fame from conversation, Truman realized he was a writer. But he was a writer who had to meet the hard standards of an acerbic critic whose last name was Capote.

My mother died in Mississippi, and I was staying for a month or so in the Yazoo Motel settling the tiny estate when I saw in the papers that Truman was giving the main lecture at the Mississippi Arts Festival in Jackson the next afternoon. I needed to get out of town.

I drove the forty-odd miles to Jackson and arrived a few minutes early, posting myself at the back stage entrance to the auditorium on the Millsaps campus.

Momentarily a large limousine pulled up. Truman was in it, surrounded by several literary matrons in hats. He was looking glum—*trapped* may be a better word—and was perhaps rather drunk. Then suddenly he sighted me, and his expression was transmuted.

"There's Willie Morris!" he shouted. "Oh, boy!"

He embraced me, an inebriated little bear dressed up for a literary reading. "What in the *world* are *you* doing here?" Afterwards, in the bar of his motel, the lady and her handsome young daughter who were accompanying him the next day to Los Angeles (he was trying to get the young daughter a modeling job in Beverly Hills) left us to our talk.

A middle-aged woman with purple hair from Alabama came to our table.

"Mr. Capote, I read that book *In Cold Blood*. I just have one question. Did you personally know them two *murderers?*"

"Madame," he said, "did I know them? I lived with them for seven *years.*"

In his motel room that night, before I left to drive back to Yazoo City, he lay on the bed drinking straight from a fifth of Smirnoff. The young model held a cold washrag on his head. She took me to a corner of the room and whispered: "Where did he get that bottle?" Then she returned to the bed. "Try to get some sleep, Truman," she said.

"*Sleep!*" he said. "Two thousand people heard me today for five grand. And this man's momma died. And you say *sleep?*"

In his final days, he would come into a bar on Long Island called Bobby Van's to drink and pass out. Bobby's was the gathering spot for the painters and writers who had come to the vicinity over the years, and for the local people who joined us there in bemused comradeship—a mahogany bar and Tiffany lamps, checkered tablecloths, and a baby grand on which Bobby often played Cole Porter and Gershwin tunes. Sometimes Truman started drinking at noon, other times in late afternoon or early evening. Usually, he was by himself.

The cops were always picking him up for DWIs, expired licenses, and unregistered cars. There were dents in his big Buick. In his lucid moments, he would talk with us of his most dramatic conflicts with people. He had turned on those who owned yachts. The big rich did not answer their own prayers. When four excerpts from *Answered Prayers*—a roman à clef of the rich and powerful with names and addresses unchanged—appeared in *Esquire*, his former friends had spurned him.

Those of us who cared for Truman had something of a proprietary feeling for him. I think we felt his extraordinary tenderness and self-destructive vulnerability, and we worried a little for him, for he often seemed lost and afraid. I drove him home from Bobby Van's a number of times. One heard the roar of the ocean from his house. He would sit in an enormous sofa much too big for him. One afternoon of snow and high winds he brought out an unopened pint of seventy-five-year-old bourbon that he said he had bought at an auction for $300. When I took a sip, I could feel it in my toes. Truman drank most of it, and it enhanced his stories. But as the stories wound down, he would sink into his sofa, a small man, alone. "I have too many houses in too many places," he would complain then, and he would number his various establishments on his fingers. When I admired one of his paperweights on the coffee table, he said: "Isak Dinesen gave it to me. It's yours. Please." I refused. "If not, never speak to me again." He gave wristwatches to people he trusted, he said. Why not paperweights?

The last time I was with him was at a noontime Sunday of early spring in Bobby Van's. The lilacs were out, and Bill Styron and I were at the bar when Truman came in alone and took his front table at the window overlooking the sidewalk. Bill and I went to pay our respects.

"Lunch is on me," Truman said. "Pull up a chair."

He was at his best—funny, charming, and effusive. He was glad to see us, and he regaled us with stories. He was close to finishing *Answered Prayers*, he said, between his vodkas. He was in the middle of a memoir for *Playboy*, he told us, of his late friend and adversary Tennessee Williams. He had just finished a paragraph that morning about Tennessee, he said, and he began to quote it to us. As he talked, I was reminded of an earlier moment, also in Bobby Van's, but with James Jones at my side instead of Styron. In the dying sunlight, Jones and I had sat mesmerized as Truman, in his wide-brimmed hat, began telling us, in the most graphic detail, all about his family from Alabama. I had never once heard him open himself so like that, about his parents, aunts, uncles, cousins, and himself there in the South. We learned that his mother had once been "Miss Alabama" years before she committed suicide, and that one of his cousins was a professional parachute jumper. To some, it may have seemed incongruous that the lisping little fellow with the wide-brimmed hat could talk so easily, so comfortably with the supposedly macho, busted-down sergeant James Jones about Alabamian aunts and uncles—and about his time in the French Quarter in New Orleans, and the months he spent in the motel room in Garden City, Kansas. And it may have seemed equally incongruous that Jones would listen. But there was nothing extraordinary about the easy conversation; the men who wrote *In Cold Blood* and *The Thin Red Line* knew mutually of life's shadings and extremes.

Remembering now that last time, when Truman shared his table with a boy from Mississippi and a boy from Virginia, I understand the truth of what Styron later said about our host: "Here was an artist of my age who could make words dance and sing, change color mysteriously, perform feats of magic, provoke laughter, send a chill up the back, touch the heart—a full-fledged master of the language before he was old enough to vote." I also understand the truth of what Truman once told me in Bobby Van's: "All Southerners go home sooner or later," he said, "even if in a box."

Truman did not make it in the box; his ashes now rest in Long Island. But I feel that on that afternoon in Bobby Van's he had already returned home. He was telling stories, alive to the power of the word, living the life he had learned in Monroeville, Alabama. I wish to remember Truman in just this way—the exuberant, witty, brave, and outrageous observer of the human parade in its foibles, of the people passing by. That is the true Truman Capote, the one that no tawdry memoirs or tales of dissolution can diminish, the one that readers meet every time they examine the finely honed phrases of "A Tree of Night" or "Children On Their Birthdays." That was Truman Capote the writer, my friend, and a man I miss.

The Epistolary Soldier

Jim Jones and I were comrades and neighbors in the last years of his life, after he and Gloria and the children returned to America from Paris and settled in our village by the sea on eastern Long Island. He was a loyal friend and a memorable companion. These were the years that he was struggling against his own death to finish the concluding volume, *Whistle*, of his monumental trilogy of men-at-war which began with *From Here to Eternity* and continued with *The Thin Red Line*.

To Reach Eternity contains the rich and revealing letters of Jim Jones. He was a complex and deeply feeling man who spoke honestly and knew what he was talking about. In reading these letters, selected and edited by George Hendrick of the University of Illinois with resourceful, descriptive, biographical bridges. I acknowledge anew how serious and impassioned Jim was about being a writer, that it was his whole life: "serious about fiction in a way that now seems a little old-fashioned and ingenuous," his old friend William Styron writes in an eloquent and moving Foreword, "with the novel for him in magisterial reign."

So profound was Jim's dedication that only three days before he died in 1977 he dictated into a tape-recorder in the heart ward at the Southampton hospital the final passage of *Whistle*, including the suicide of his character, Strange: "He had taken into himself all the pain and anguish and sorrow and misery that is the lot of all soldiers." He never wrote a more autobiographical sentence.

He was born in 1921 in Robinson, Illinois, growing up in his words "in an atmosphere of hot emotions and boiling recriminations covered with a thin but resilient skin of gentility." His family was an old and prominent one which had fallen on hard days. His father was an alcoholic dentist who killed himself.

There was no money for college. Jim enlisted in the army in 1939 and was stationed in Hawaii. In his spare hours he read most of the books in the post library and took courses at the University of Hawaii. "I stumbled onto the works of Thomas Wolfe, and his home life sounded so similar to my own, his feelings about himself so similar to mine about myself, that I realized I had been a writer all my life without knowing it or having written." Given his burgeoning sensibilities, he was unique witness to the extraordinary caste system of the United States pre-war army, the uncommon American proletariat, the castoffs and misfits like Prewitt and Maggio, the fear and brutality. In an early letter to his brother Jeff:

> [In the post theatre] the officers' children . . . sit in the balcony. We common herd sit in the "pit" as the rabble did in Shakespeare's day also. We are not allowed to associate with the officers' children at all. I was told of a fella who was running around with an officer's daughter here about a year ago, and he laid her. She had a baby, and he is still serving his year in the guardhouse. Another boy was walking down a walk and a little girl skating past him fell down. He picked her up. The girl thanked him, but the sergeant who saw him got him a month in the "little red schoolhouse."

He began writing in Hawaii. "I'm writing in the dark all the time. . . . If only some authority that knew would tell [me] I was good and had promise, then I'd be all right, but as it is, I'm always full of that fear that maybe I'm not very good. Sometimes I get so damned low I feel like blowing my brains out. That's no shit, it's the straight dope." Never a refined stylist, certainly not in the conventional sense, he struggled to find a voice, and when the war came he harbored a deeper fear. "I might be dead in a month, which would mean that I would never learn how to say and never get said those things which proved I had once existed somewhere."

War would remain the very substance of his life, the sustaining reality he wrote the best about. He was obsessed, for instance, with our own Civil War, the slaughter and blindness and terrible caprice of it. One springtime, a year before his death, he and I took our teenaged sons, David and Jamie, to the Civil War battlefields below Washington, ending at the tormented ground of Antietam, scene of the bloodiest single day's combat in the history of warfare. Jim and I concluded that day that if we had been living then, we would have fought on different sides. It was

raining heavily and the four of us returned to our motel at Harper's
Ferry. Jim dropped us there, then went back to Antietam by himself. He
returned three hours later, soaking wet. Why did he go back in such
weather? I asked him. "There are places a man has to be alone," he
replied.

From Hawaii in '42 Jim shipped with the First Army to Guadalcanal,
where he was in vicious hand-to-hand combat. A starved Japanese soldier
slipped out of the jungle and attacked him while he was relieving himself.
He had to kill the soldier. This haunted him for years. To his brother
Jeff from Guadalcanal in '43:

> You don't spend any time in consoling yourself that if you die, you will
> be dying for your country and Liberty and Democracy and Freedom,
> because after you are dead, there is no such thing as Liberty or Democracy
> or Freedom. It's impossible to look at things thru the viewpoint of the
> group rather than your individual eyes. The group means nothing to you
> if you cannot remain a part of it. But in spite of all this, you keep on
> fighting because you know that there is nothing else for you to do.

He was wounded in action, then badly reinjured an ankle, and was
eventually evacuated to Kennedy General Hospital in Memphis. The
scenes of that booming wartime city, the booze and the girls and the
embittered fellow wounded, psychologically scarred by war, would later
provide him with many of the indelible episodes of *Whistle*.

Twice he went AWOL. On one trip over the hill to his hometown in
Illinois, he met a forceful and eccentric married woman named Lowney
Handy, who conducted a bizarre writers' colony in the woods. She encouraged him in his writing and reading. When he was mustered out of
the Army with an honorable discharge they began an affair which lasted
for years.

Jim moved to New York and enrolled in writing courses at N.Y.U.
He finished a war novel called *They Shall Inherit the Laughter*. Without
an appointment he turned up in the legendary Maxwell Perkins's office at
Scribner's with the manuscript in a hatbox. He knew Perkins was the
editor of Wolfe, Hemingway, Fitzgerald, and Lardner. Perkins did not
accept the novel, but was absorbed by a paragraph in a covering letter

that Jim's next book would pertain to life in the pre-war Army. Perkins gave him a $500 advance on what was to become *Eternity*.

Some of the most intriguing of Jim's letters are to Perkins, who died before the completion of *Eternity*, and to Perkins's successor, Burroughs Mitchell—candid and moving letters about writing and literature. To Mitchell on Perkins's death in '47: "I have had the feeling for a long time that I should come to New York, that he might die, that I should not selfishly but for writing go where he was because there was so much that I could learn from him. But as I said, life does not ever put two such things together; his time of that was with Tom Wolfe and not with me."

He worked for five years on *Eternity*, traveling across America in a jeep and trailer which Lowney Handy's husband had bought him, stopping for long periods in trailer camps from Florida to Arizona. It was not easy for him. "For almost four solid years," he wrote Mitchell in '47, "I've done nothing much but write and haven't earned a penny at it, and have not published a word, and see no immediate prospect of doing so. Truly, there seems to be no place at all in our society for the artist who is really in earnest. And all the dumbjohns always hollering about what's wrong with art in our time." Anyone who has just completed a novel which has seemed such lonely and unending and wounding labor might appreciate how he felt on finally finishing *Eternity:* "I am like a rubber band that has been stretched over two nails for a long time and left there; you take it down from the nails and it hangs together all right. But if you try to stretch it again, even the least tiniest bit, it will crumble. Not snap, or break, or burst, or pop. Crumble."

Literally overnight he was rich and famous, having achieved what Styron in his Foreword concedes all writers secretly yearn for: commercial *and* critical success. He came to New York for these halcyon days, making the literary rounds with Bill Styron and Norman Mailer and his other fellow writers of that day. "I guess I'm really a provincial at heart," he wrote Lowney Handy, "but I guess everybody is, who is honest. I have been using your technique of the cornfed boy fresh in the city since I got here and can get anything I want from anybody."

Next was *Some Came Running*, savaged by the critics, and then *The Pistol*, which he claimed to have done to show the reviewers he could write straight and lyrical English. He broke with Lowney and married

Gloria Mossolini, a beautiful young actress and fledgling writer, and they moved to Paris. From these European years came some good work, and some questionable, but preeminently what might have been his life's masterpiece, the Guadalcanal combat novel *The Thin Red Line*, about which Romain Gary would comment: "It is essentially an epic love poem about the human predicament and like all great books it leaves one with a feeling of wonder and hope."

Jim and Gloria returned from Europe to Sagaponack, Long Island, in 1972 and bought an old farmhouse there. It was surrounded by potato fields and they christened it "Chateau Spud." They wanted their children to go to American schools, and both Kaylie and Jamie attended East Hampton High. Jim wrote a splendid personal and historical text to an illustrated book, *WWII*, among his best words, but mostly he was giving himself to *Whistle*. Until he grew seriously ill these were good years for him. He had always been achingly American, and he loved watching his children grow up in that milieu, relished too the lunches at Bobby Van's in Bridgehampton, our beach cookouts and softball games and leisurely dinners with close friends in his grand country kitchen. Some nights he would bring out one of his big Padron cigars and read us aloud from his work that day on *Whistle*. Gloria is one of the great women of America, and their marriage was without peer the best I have ever seen.

As a man Jim had a dark view of human life, its cruelties and shames, which he expressed in his fiction. He had little patience with the glib and easy optimisms; existence was too dire and complex for that. "That's the perennial problem of a writer: of distinguishing between true affirmation, which is not sentimental, and the false affirmation parroted by all the affirmation-shouters, which is so sentimental it makes you sick to hear it. There is no reason that I can see at present why we should smugly believe that we will endure—and prevail—just because we are men."

All this may seem discordant, his old editor Burroughs Mitchell observed, with his personal life in his adult years, "a vigorously enjoyed life, filled with family happiness and many friendships," in which a man like Jim "will try exceptionally hard to make the most of every good thing he can find in his lifetime." He was happy on having returned home.

As the end approached he worked harder than any writer I had ever known, sometimes ten or twelve hours a day in his attic above the potato fields with the distant prospect of the ocean beyond. Sometimes I had a deep, secret intuition that he did not really want to finish *Whistle*, that the killing off of the old infantry company was coincident and a presage of his own death. Yet he fought to the finish, and those of us who knew and loved him then honored him for it.

Twelve years now after his death, I sense that Jim's hard-earned work is rightfully taking its place in the pantheon of American letters. Among its other attributes, this collection should serve as an invaluable example to aspiring writers: the hard work, the loneliness, the heart's commitment.

"I would like to leave books behind me," he wrote to his brother as early as '42, "to let people know that I have lived. I'd like to think that people would read them avidly, as I have read so many and would feel the sadness and frustration and joy and love I tried to put in them, that people would think about that guy James Jones and wish they had known that guy who could write like that." He believed this. "I write," he once told an interviewer, "to reach eternity."

In the Spirit of the Game

This is a tale not of one Game Day but two, because each was deeply enmeshed in the other.

It begins with the Ole Miss–Vanderbilt game of October 28, 1989, in Oxford, Mississippi. It was Ole Miss Homecoming, one of those Southern autumn days touched with the airy bittersweet languor of the past and memory and childhood . . . and football.

Ole Miss is small by measure with other state universities, with 10,000 students—roughly the same population as the town—who are suffused with the flamboyant élan of their contemporaries everywhere. In moments there is a palpable, affecting sophistication to its stunningly beautiful campus in the rolling rural woodlands of the South. On this homecoming day, one might recall Thomas Wolfe's only slightly fictional Pulpit Hill, patterned after the Chapel Hill of many years ago in *Look Homeward, Angel:* "There was still a good flavor of the wilderness about the place—one felt its remoteness, its isolated charm. It seemed to Eugene like a provincial outpost of great Rome: The wilderness crept up to it like a beast."

Two hours before the kickoff, the young men of the Ole Miss team, led by Coach Billy "Dog" Brewer, walked single file through the Grove, a huge old verdant circle only a stone's throw from the stadium, as avid tailgaters applauded. From the distance the band played "From Dixie with Love," a blended rendition of "Dixie" and "The Battle Hymn of the Republic." As the mighty sounds wafted across this wooded terrain, little girls in the school's Harvard red and Yale blue tossed and leapt, and miniature quarterbacks in replica jerseys threw footballs to incipient Rebel wide receivers. The adults were drinking, and everywhere was the ineffable cachet of fried chicken and barbecue. On one lengthy table draped with a vintage Delta tablecloth were eight-branch silver candelabra with red taper candles and mounds of food on matching silver trays.

On another was a substantial arrangement of flowers flowing out of an Ole Miss football helmet—lacy white fragile baby's-breath and red carnations.

The stadium itself, surrounded by its young magnolias, was cozy and contained, and much removed from the mega-stadiums of the SEC behemoths Alabama and Auburn and Tennessee and Georgia and LSU and Florida. Its grassy turf had seen Bruiser Kinard, Charlie Conerly, Barney Poole, Jake Gibbs, Squirrel Griffin, Gene Hickerson, Archie Manning, and Gentle Ben Williams. There were 34,500 in attendance on this afternoon, including a smattering of Vandy partisans down from Tennessee in their bright-gold colors matching the golden patina of this day. At Ole Miss, *The New York Times* would report of what was to follow, "The game blends into the dense history of a school that has often played out the richest and darkest passions of the region."

There is a special flavor, a texture, to Deep Southern collegiate football, and this was best expressed years ago by Marino Casem, the longtime coach at Alcorn University: "In the East college football is a cultural exercise. On the West coast it is a tourist attraction. In the Midwest it is cannibalism. But in the Deep South it is religion, and Saturday is the holy day."

There was indeed a religiosity to this crowd in the moments before game time. In the south end zone a loyalist group perennially regarded as The Rowdies, a perfervid cadre consisting of professors, bartenders, writers, and reprobates, shouted epithets at the visitors down from their cerebral Nashville halls: "Down with the Eggheads! Stomp the Existentialists!" A Yankee reporter, surveying this end zone phalanx, asked one of its number, Dean Faulkner Wells, niece of the hometown bard, why she supported Ole Miss football. With a succinctness uncharacteristic of the Faulkner breed, she replied: "Continuity."

The record of the Ole Miss team at this juncture was five wins, two losses. It was hobbled with injuries. At one point the entire starting defensive backfield was down, including football and academic All-America safety Todd Sandroni, who was playing on one good leg. The Rebels' largest margin of victory had been seven points. They had upset Florida on the road by four while gaining only 128 offensive yards. They had defeated Georgia on a touchdown pass with thirty-one seconds to go in this stadium, and Tulane on another pass in New Orleans with four seconds remaining. It was a funny, gritty ball club, small and hurt in the mighty SEC, a ball club people could not help but love.

There was 6:57 left in the first quarter when it happened.

Vandy faced third and goal from the Ole Miss 12 in a scoreless game. Quarterback John Gromos faded for the pass. Brad Gaines, the 210-pound fullback, caught it on the two.

Roy Lee "Chucky" Mullins, the 175-pound Ole Miss cornerback, suddenly raced across the field, leapt high, and tackled the receiver, forcing him to drop the football. The resounding thud could be heard for yards around. Cheers rolled across the stadium. But Mullins lay prone on the field, and when he did not move, a fateful quiet descended.

"I couldn't get off the sideline," Ole Miss coach Dog Brewer would later recall. "In all the years I've been coaching, it's the first time I haven't gone on the field when there was a serious injury. I couldn't go. I thought the kid was dead. No matter how long I coach, I'll always remember how he came flying through the air and made that hit—the thud of it."

The silent throng watched as the trainers and doctor cut Mullins's face mask away and strapped him to a wooden board. It took them more than ten horrible minutes. Then they carried him to the opposite sidelines, and the ambulance slowly wound its way out of the stadium toward the hospital. The scene would not easily be obliterated.

The rest of the first half seemed bitter anticlimax. The flat, listless Ole Miss team fell behind 10–0. Chucky Mullins's injury likewise cast an ominous pall over the homecoming rituals of halftime, the Ole Miss beauties in evening dresses, the playing of the alma mater.

How to explain such human moments? Ole Miss came out in the third quarter on fire, then erupted in the fourth. Trailing 17–16, Ole Miss took over on its own 21 with 9:18 remaining. Halfback Tyrone Ashley carried twice for 13 yards, then quarterback John Darnell hit tight end Rick Gebbia of Long Island ("our own Yankee") for 49 yards to the Commodore 17. On the ensuing play Ashley broke free for the winning touchdown with 7:18 left. The game ended 24–17.

In the locker room the Ole Miss players were choked up over their fallen teammate. There was no celebration after this one.

Sometime in the second half Chucky had been flown to Memphis, seventy-five miles away. The small hospital in Oxford could do little but stabilize his condition. He lay now in neurosurgery intensive care in the Baptist Memorial Hospital.

He was paralyzed from the neck down. The injury was serious, with little likelihood that he would ever recover. The attending doctors would call it one of the most drastic injuries they had ever seen, likening the impact that crushed his back to the crushing of an empty can. The vertebrae had exploded; there was nothing left. On the Monday after homecoming four surgeons performed a three-hour operation using wire and bone graft from Chucky's pelvis to fuse the shattered vertebrae. He would remain a quadriplegic.

The mood of the university, the town, and the state in the following days was of grief and sadness. Ole Miss dedicated the rest of the season to him.

In 1987 Chucky Mullins, a seventeen-year-old from the tiny town of Russellville, in northwest Alabama, came to Ole Miss, one of many poor young blacks signed each year by the Rebels. When he was recruited and given an athletic scholarship, he did not have the money to get to Oxford. His mother had died, so he was raised by a legal guardian, a young man who suffered from a debilitating lung disease. In his senior year in high school, Chucky was the football captain. Both Auburn and Alabama considered him too small and slow, and he wanted to go to Ole Miss.

He was Dog Brewer's kind of athlete: "He was lanky, always clapping, having fun, what we call a 'glue' player, not that fast or big, but the kind that holds a team together. What you saw him wearing was damn near what he owned. But to see him, you'd think he was a millionaire."

Chucky's best friend on the Ole Miss team was a white freshman named Trea Southerland. After the operation in Memphis two days after the Vandy game, Chucky came out of the anesthesia whispering Southerland's name. "Chucky added a lot to other people's lives," Southerland said. "And I know that if desire and character make a difference, he'll find a way to beat this."

A chance photograph before the Vanderbilt homecoming game had caught a pristine moment. Coach Brewer and Mullins are standing together in the north end zone, not far from where Chucky would soon be hurt, the coach's arm around number 38's waist as the two of them lead the team onto the field. It was a gesture of symbolic affinity: Brewer was also from a poor family and a broken home, attending Ole Miss in its glory days as a "step slow" ball player. "When you love the game, it has a hold on you," Brewer says of Mullins, but it is an autobiographical confession too. "I kind of saw myself in him. The only way out for both of us was football."

Ole Miss was matched the next Saturday against the Bayou Bengals of LSU. For the first time since 1960, this tumultuous and historic rivalry would be played in Oxford.

Within hours of Chucky Mullins's injury a trust fund had been started for him. LSU collected donations at its Purple-Gold basketball game in Baton Rouge. The University of Delaware shut down a football practice an hour early for a prayer session. Calls from coaches—and the White House—came in from all over America. Coach Bill Curry, then of Alabama, collected donations from his players. "Statistics tell us," Curry said, "that football is a very safe game when you're talking about catastrophic injuries. Ankles? Knees? Fingers? No, it's not safe. But not one time in a billion do you see the kind of injury that happened to Chucky Mullins."

Mike Archer, the LSU coach, visited Chucky in the hospital Friday night before the Saturday game. "I can understand how this has affected their team," he said. "I almost broke down with tears when I visited with him. It hurts to see a strong, healthy kid like that, so young."

Shortly before the game, seven Ole Miss men in the finals for "Colonel Reb," the campus's highest accolade, withdrew from the election and swung the honor to Mullins.

The LSU match would be one of the most dramatic moments in Ole Miss sports annals. The Rebel players wore number 38 on their helmets. The largest crowd in the history of the little stadium, 42,354, turned out for the contest. Hundreds of Ole Miss students volunteered to pass buckets during the game for the trust fund. More than $240,000 would be collected at this game alone, five times more than the goal.

Chucky Mullins was listening on the radio in the intensive care unit in Memphis. Just prior to the kickoff there was a prayer for his welfare.

The Vandy victory the previous Saturday had given 6–2 Ole Miss an opportunity at the SEC title and a chance at its first Sugar Bowl since 1970. Yet devastation struck the Rebels early, and it was obvious that they were taut with emotion—fumbles, incomplete passes, penalties. LSU quarterback Tom Hodson was magnificent, and the Tigers jumped to a swift 21–0 lead. The score was 35–10 late in the third period, and the LSU depth was showing.

Then, suddenly, as they had all year against adversity, the Rebels, outweighed and outmanned at nearly every position, crippled by injury and despair, came alive in the final quarter. Quarterback Darnell's formerly errant passes began to click, and slashing runs by sophomores Randy Baldwin and Tyrone Ashley left gaping holes in the Louisiana phalanx. The Rebel players were yelling to each other after each big play: "This one's for Chucky! We're gonna do it!"

The score was now LSU 35, Ole Miss 30. The Rebels were driving from their own territory as the game ebbed away. A burnt orange sun was descending behind Vaught-Hemingway Stadium, and the air was eerie with the early dark. The entire assemblage was on its feet, and the partisan fans were stomping in unison, filling the hazy mystic afternoon with the pandemonium of fealty.

Twenty-five seconds remained now, and the Rebels had first and 10 on the LSU 30. Quarterback Darnell, injured five plays before, limped back onto the field. An uncommon hush descended, and a member of the south end zone Rowdies fell out of a lower row of the bleachers.

As the play unfolded, Darnell hobbled back into the pocket. The nimble wide receiver, Willie Green, streaked toward the south end zone, covered only by cornerback Jimmy Young, four inches shorter. It only took seconds. The ball was in flight now, suspended it seemed for the briefest eternity etched against the waning horizon, as Willie Green leapt high, arms outraised in one quick pirouette of hope.

The pass came up two feet short. The Bayou Bengals defender, high in the air with Green, intercepted in the end zone, then fell lovingly to the turf, ball in breast.

If the Rebels had scored, they would have led 36–35 with 20 seconds left. Going for and making the two-point conversion, they would have achieved a symbolic 38.

Yet life often does not work that way. A great sporting event indeed emulates life, its ecstasies and sorrows, its gallantries and failures, and its time running out, the time that runs out in Dixie autumn twilights for all of us who wish life to give us feeling and victory and hope against old mortality. The Bayou Bengals intercepted, 20 seconds left. Only the love remained, and the possibility.

My Friend Forrest Gump

I've known Winston Groom for almost a quarter of a century, and I've learned over the years and through various mutual mischiefs that although he bears certain striking personal similarities to Forrest Gump himself, he's no idiot. He's a big, tall fellow, Southern to the core, old Mobile aristocracy, whom a girl in Elaine's in New York, back in those days when you could call a woman a girl and get away with it, insisted looked like Gary Cooper in *The Fountainhead*. I always called him "Captain" because of his combat stint in Vietnam, an appellation he asked me never to use, but I note he did not complain when during Forrest Gump Day in Mobile last year they christened a shrimpboat "the Captain Groom."

I was the first person to read the manuscript of his novel *Forrest Gump*, which he sent me in Oxford in about 1986 while I was writer-in-residence at Ole Miss, and which I liked enormously, but that is a story that requires a little background.

Winston Groom and I first met in 1974 at a saloon called Bobby Van's on the main street of Bridgehampton, on the South Fork of eastern Long Island. He was thirty-one years old. He was a reporter at the time on the old *Washington Star*, the afternoon competition to the *Post*, and was visiting his friend Adam Shaw, who also lived in Washington as a *Post* reporter (but who was vacationing with his father, Irwin Shaw, out in the Hamptons). Winston claims we left the saloon after a good long while and threw rocks at cars a half hour or so. "You were no good then," he says, "and you're no good now."

A couple of years later, our Bicentennial year, I went down to Washington to spend three months as "writer-in-residence" on the *Star*, which meant doing three columns a week at good money and on anything I wanted to write about. Winston's desk in the newsroom was next to mine. My predecessor as guest writer had been Jimmy Breslin, and rummaging through the desk drawers my first day there I came across Breslin's cigar stubs, empty whisky bottles, and dirty socks.

For those of you who have seen *All the President's Men,* I will assure you the newsroom of the old *Star* bore scant resemblance to the newsroom of the *Post* with its lush carpets and furnishings. It was, in fact, grubby. The *Star* building itself was in such a perilous neighborhood that the security guards escorted women reporters to their cars in the parking lot after dark; there had once been an armed robbery in the main lobby.

On that first day, the editor-in-chief, a resourceful fellow named Jim Bellows, assigned Winston to teach me how to use a word processor. I was grudging. "It's easy," he said petulantly. "Just look." After watching his demonstration, I said the deal was off. "How the hell did I get involved with you, Morris?" he snorted. He managed to persuade one of the veteran copy editors to take my subsequent pieces, written half on typewriter and half in longhand. They were lengthy pieces, too, and occasionally somewhat off deadline. After I had served my stretch and returned to Bridgehampton, Winston phoned to tell me my copy had driven the copy editor quite insane. He had just been decked for appending to the food editor's recipe for chocolate chip cookies the phrase "eight ounces of dog shit," which had actually appeared in the first edition.

In that most singular of newsrooms Winston and I played pranks on each other. He would add quotes from Dostoyevsky or Henry Miller or any of a number of others to my copy. Once, near deadline, he was on the telephone tracking down a late-breaking murder story, and I retired to a pay phone and called his extension and identified myself as the murderer and made a sizeable confession. When I abashedly returned to the newsroom while he was recording the confession and confessed myself, he said, accentuating every word: "Do that again on pain of death."

I had a hard time finding an apartment, and while I looked for one I stayed with his ex-wife Baba, a beautiful Alabaman from Tallassee. My immediate roommate was Fenwick—Baba and her ex-husband's big dog. Fenwick slept in the same bed with me, often lavishing me with slobbery kisses. After finishing my first column I was so debilitated by being out of practice with newspaper deadlines that Fenwick and I slept together around the clock for three days, ordering home delivery pizza which we shared. I was having second thoughts about spending three months of my life writing columns, and in the end it was Winston who persuaded me to return to work. "It's a matter of honor, damn you," he said.

Eventually, Winston found a place for me on Prince Street in Old Town Alexandria. It was a solid eighteenth-century domicile with two floors and a loft with a skylight added at the top with a ladder to get to it. In the back, beyond a patio, there was an ancient well which had once been filled in and which began collapsing shortly after I arrived. The house was the narrowest in Alexandria, only eight feet wide, and was listed as such in the Bicentennial guide to the walking tour of Old Town. The tourists, reading their guidebooks, were instructed to turn right off Royal, and then the book said: "Take a close look at 40 Prince. How wide do you think this house is?" I had a work table set up just inside the front door, and thirty or forty times a day I would hear the tourists in front of my house asking in loud tongues straight from the American suburbs and prairies and swamps and canebrakes: "How wide do you think this house is?" Consequently, I did not spend much time in there, but in Winston's place up the way with his legions of friends, mostly Southerners who threw a lot of parties, or cruising the haunted and beguiling Old Dominion countryside with them, or spending countless evenings in a minuscule French restaurant down from the White House which reminded me of La Belle Aurora in *Casablanca*, where Bogie and Bergman used to hang out and drink champagne.

Winston knew and understood Washington in its many facets and helped me with his flamboyant network of sources to find unusual people to write about in my columns, a veritable horde of the human fauna: defrocked priests who slept in firehouses, Marxist cheeseburger chefs, both varieties of AAs, housewives drifting in ennui, blacks who wanted to go back to Dixie, young women who should have stayed in Oshkosh, parking attendants who had been mugged eleven times, cabdrivers from the deepest boondocks, bookies from the James River in doubleknits, drunken linemen for the Redskins, and politicians, politicians, politicians. He put me in touch with Wilbur Mills not long after old Wilbur had jumped into the Tidal Basin with the stripper Fannie Foxx. Almost in an existential mist I absorbed this mélange, and Winston's knowledge of the town led me to sense that it was not the place it had been even as recently as eight or ten years before, but was inexorably becoming an amalgam of such places as New York and Atlanta. He himself did not relish this trend and complained that he was getting played out with Washington.

The *Star* did not have the team depth of the *Post*, but it was a good newspaper and had a flair to it (it had long since outgrown its nadir days of the mid-1940s when it had one day proclaimed in seventy-two-point banner headline, and throughout the story underneath it, the explosion of "the Atomic Bum"), with an array of fine writers and reporters that included Mary McCrory, Jack Germond, Ed Yoder, Jack Sherwood, the cartoonist Pat Oliphant, and Winston. He was a superb reporter, with a prose that was clean, flexible, and incisive. He was very intelligent and well-educated and candid, with a gift of raucous comedy that emanated from his undergraduate days as editor of the humor magazine at the University of Alabama. He was also highly disciplined, which he did not want anybody to see. I always wanted to know what he thought about things. He always had a fresh angle on life, although he was becoming jaded about newspapering. It is a tough, demanding business, and he thought he was not accomplishing anything that mattered. In our cups on late-nights he began telling me about his experiences as an infantry lieutenant in Vietnam. He had gone there out of ROTC at 'Bama and served mostly with the Fourth Infantry Division. His stories were lucid, compelling, ironic. If I have ever done anything smart in my life, it was to convince him to leave the newspaper and write his Vietnam novel, that if he did not write it soon he might never write it. At first he was skeptical, but finally he took the plunge. With his severance pay from the *Star* he moved out to our vicinity on Long Island to write the book. I admired the passages he showed me in those months. But it was a cold winter, the book had not been sold, and he was running out of money.

Writers lived in our neighborhood: Truman Capote, Irwin Shaw, Joseph Heller, Peter Matthiessen, Kurt Vonnegut, Jr., and in the cruel winters there was a community among us out there. Our friend, James Jones, who had returned with his family to America from years in Paris and was struggling against death to finish *Whistle*, the third novel in his World War II trilogy, was a generous man and especially helpful to Winston. Their war experiences contributed to their friendship. When I was doing a memoir of Jim Jones after his death, I asked Winston to put

down for me the specific ways in which Jim had advised him, and he
wrote:

> Jim had taken immediate interest in the book. The first time we talked
> about it he thought over the brief story line I told him and handed out the
> following advice: "Whoever this main character of yours is, I think you
> should make him as different from yourself as possible. There'll be enough
> similarities anyway, but I'd make him different so far as background and
> looks and everything else." He would always ask about the book. He
> wanted to know about the characters and what was going on. He asked to
> see a copy of the first hundred pages and after he'd read them he called
> up and asked me to come over. We sat around that big kitchen table one
> afternoon, just the two of us. "I'm going to show you a few things," he
> said. We spent an hour, or maybe more, going over some pages. They
> were subtle, marvelous techniques he'd learned over the years. "If you
> lop off this sentence and make it a separate paragraph here, it gives a
> punch to the scene," he'd say. Or, "Instead of having this character tell
> this part of the story, just take his best quotes and use them and tell the
> rest in third person. It saves half the space." He said: "One of the hardest
> things to do is to show something about one character by having another
> character think about what the first character is thinking or might be
> thinking. I'm trying to do that now, in *Whistle,* and I ain't done it before.
> But it's a damned good device." We had a couple of those sessions and
> each time I came away with something I didn't know before.

Winston was working away on his book, and I on one of mine, and
there were good moments to be had, too. The eastern end of Long Island,
when one lived there year round, bore little resemblance in the 1970s to
the Hamptons of the summer society columns of the latter day. In the
off-season it was still a quintessentially rural place with a quiet village
life—anything but a "writers' colony," thank God for that. It was the
beauty of the earth which helped hold us together: potato fields on the
flat land, village greens, old graveyards drowsing in the sun, shingled
houses, ancient elms along muted lanes, snow drifts on the sand dunes,
and, far in the distance, the blue Atlantic breakers. The villages themselves, among the oldest in America, remained part of the land which

encompassed them. It was a place of bleak snows and tormenting winds, of long nights and silences.

Adam Shaw had also left the Washington newspaper cosmos to write a book, and he, Winston, and I were constant companions. Bobby Van's saloon was an angular structure on the main street of our adopted village with dark paneling, Tiffany lamps, and old fans suspended from an undistinguished ceiling, a long mahogany bar, and from the back the flickering candles on small booths and tables with red checkered tablecloths—then, too, a covered porch outside named "Nematode Hall" after our summer softball team, the Golden Nematodes. Winston and Adam (who we called "Swiss" because he was born in Switzerland) and I usually put up work around seven in the evening and met here for drinks and dinner, sometimes to hear Truman Capote's tales of his unusual Southern relatives, or Irwin Shaw's stories of his World War II days as a soldier in Europe, including the one about the day in Paris in August 1945, when he and his pal Ernest Hemingway liberated the Ritz Bar. Sometimes we played Monopoly with Jim Jones and his kids at his farmhouse surrounded by potato fields. May I reveal that the author of *From Here to Eternity* sometimes cheated at Monopoly? Winston listened closely to these older writers, absorbing their casual talk about the craft. He reminded me not too long ago that I kept the whole neighborhood up on these nights by trying to play "Taps" on a battered old bugle that belonged to Jim Jones. "What came out," he recalled, "sounded more like 'The Song of the Vulgar Boatmen' than anything else."

Since they knew I always slept till noon, Winston and Swiss frequently crept up to the window of the bedroom of my house on Church Lane at nine or ten a.m., pounding on the screen and making vociferous howls to wake me up. This backfired one day, however. I was up and around uncharacteristically early and in the bathroom. They whacked on the bathroom window. "You've made me cut myself shaving!" I shouted, then hastened into the adjacent kitchen, applied a copious amount of tomato ketchup to my throat, and lay down on the floor. They burst in through the kitchen door and looked down as I made gurgling noises. "My God!" Winston shouted. "The SOB's cut his jugular." They never tried to wake me up again.

Jim Jones died of congestive heart failure in 1977. Winston and I phoned an assistant to Ted Kennedy in Washington for help in getting an accomplished Army bugler to play "Taps" at Jim's service in Bridgehampton. We asked for a private who also was a career soldier. An officer in the Department of the Army telephoned shortly. They had a career soldier, he said, but he was not a private. "All the best buglers these days are master sergeants," he explained. The officer went on to say that his man was not only the best damned bugler in the U.S. Army, but the best bugler in the world. "He's played at the graves of three presidents. And he volunteered for this assignment. He's right here." Master Sergeant Mastroleo came on the line. He admired Mr. Jones, he said—he remembered Montgomery Clift as the bugler Prewitt in *From Here to Eternity*. He flew from Washington and spent the night before the funeral in the adjacent wing of the house Winston and Swiss were renting. That evening after dinner Winston and I and some friends wept as we heard the sergeant in the back yard practicing the notes to his "Taps," the mournful strains of it wafting over the tranquil ponds and inlets and pines to the ocean beyond.

Jim's death affected Winston deeply. His subsequent dedication to his Vietnam novel read: "For two soldiers—my father, who served in a different war in different times; and James Jones."

Better Times Than These came out in 1978. In every way it was a big book, written on a large scale. The title derived from a song of the Seventh Cavalry Regiment, the same regiment George Armstrong Custer took to the Little Big Horn a century before.

> *There'll be better times than these,*
> *In the Seventh Cavalry,*
> *Just you wait and see, Garry Owen!*

The narrative takes the men of Bravo Company of the contemporary Seventh Cav from its journey across the Pacific in a troop transport, into the jungles and combat. The combat scenes are excruciatingly vivid. It was a story of adversity and sacrifice and redemption, the old themes of literature, told by a young writer who understood his civilization and his time without illusion—an American novel of integrity and feeling. Irwin Shaw's jacket blurb described it as "a robust, earthy account of how a group of young Americans fought the pitiless war in Vietnam. It manages to be funny, tragic, enlightening, chilling in its description of how the army actually worked during those painful years."

It was clear that Winston could write complex, ambitious fiction. It was generally well-received by the critics; it sold 60,000 copies in hardback.

In the intervening years Winston published *Only,* an affecting memoir based on his dog Fenwick, my old roommate in Alexandria; *Conversations with the Enemy,* interviews with former Vietcong soldiers; and *As Summers Die,* a novel set in the Mobile vicinity, where he had returned to live.

I came back permanently to my native Mississippi to be writer-in-residence at Ole Miss. One day out of the blue a bulky package came to my cottage on the Ole Miss campus from Winston in Mobile containing the unfinished manuscript of a novel. The book had almost been writing itself, he said in his letter. "I'm excited about it, but is it any good?" The frontispiece quote from Dryden leapt out at me: "There is a pleasure sure in being mad which none but madmen know"—then the first paragraph.

> Let me say this: bein a idiot is no box of chocolates. People laugh, lose patience, treat you shabby. Now they say folks sposed to be kind to the afflicted, but let me tell you—it ain't always that way. Even so, I got no complaints, cause I reckon I done live a pretty interestin life, so to speak.

I stayed up all night reading the manuscript. The book unfolded for me and was the genuine thing to me: a work of power, comedy, and truth. Only the Winston Groom I knew could have written it. *Forrest Gump* was published the following year to excellent reviews and modest sales: 30,000 in hardback.

Over time I could not help but reflect on the creator and the character themselves, for people have asked me. The creator does not always do what he is told, as the character does, and is in fact one of the stubbornest souls I have ever known in regard to false counsels and empty-headed instructions. But as with the character, the creator in his indwelling heart is honest, intrepid, loyal and true, esteems comradeship, places high standards on his fellows yet will be obliging to all sorts of mountebanks, fakirs and charlatans, and disfavors above all the gratuitous cruelties.

On one of Winston's later trips to Oxford he brought with him a young Mississippi beauty, Anne-Clinton Bridges, who he had met in Mobile. She had grown up in the river town of Greenville, Mississippi, where years before her grandmother had been Shelby Foote's first serious girlfriend. I could tell Winston was serious about Anne-Clinton, too. He told me he was originally drawn to her because he had grown tired of dating women who hated their mothers. They eventually married. It was a worthy choice for both of them; they mutually loved literature, dogs, and fun.

In the fall of '93 I had some book signings in Mobile and stayed two or three days in Winston and Anne-Clinton's house on the Magnolia River about twenty miles from town. It was a distinctly Deep Southern domicile, which Winston himself designed, with a broad front veranda and a lush sloping lawn that led down to the river—the only postal route in the United States where the mail was delivered daily by boat. They had a sheepdog named Forrest Gump who reminded me of his predecessor Fenwick. It was easy here to discern Winston's Old Mobile origins, his sense of place, his fond attachment to the bays and inlets and marshlands of the Bay vicinity, the shrimpboat culture, the hunting and fishing. Most of the people at a party in the house one evening were friends going back to his childhood, everybody dining on Anne-Clinton's homemade bread and indigenous gumbo, the Atlanta Braves on a television, the host and his Mobile comrades picking on guitars, a shimmering Gulf moon on the Magnolia River, and the sheepdog Forrest, inspiriting and ubiquitous.

Paramount bought the film rights to *Forrest Gump* for $300,000, plus three percent of the movie's net profits. Sitting on the back porch one night, Winston said he had seen portions of the screenplay and was concerned with the veracity of certain scenes. He had expressed this concern to the moviemakers.

Not long after that, over the July 4th weekend last year, Winston and Anne-Clinton spent a couple of days with my wife JoAnne and me in Jackson, Mississippi. They could not attend the world première of the movie, which was taking place in Hollywood one of the nights they were here. Winston had not seen the movie nor heard much from any of the people who had. On the morning they were about to drive back to Mobile, we were perusing the Sunday *New York Times* in my back yard. "Oh my God!" Winston said, "What have we here?" gesturing to a full-page ad with a lengthy roster of rave reviews from the advance screenings.

Several days later he phoned from Mobile. "You won't believe what's happening," he said. "People love it. I feel like I've been hit by a ton of shit." He still had not seen the movie, and would not until Paramount gave him a Mobile première a week or so later, complete with his friends for a private theatre party.

The movie *Forrest Gump* quickly became an American phenomenon. Children of my neighbors in Jackson went to see it three times in one week. When I saw it in Jackson, the overflow audience stood and applauded at the end. It was a prime and uncharacteristic example of a fine book being done justice to by Hollywood. It eventually became the fourth largest grossing movie ever. The novel, brought back in print not long before the movie, had by January, 1995 sold 1.5 million copies.

A month or so after the release of the movie JoAnne and I drove to the mountains of North Carolina, down in the southwest corner of the state, where Anne-Clinton and Winston were renting a house at the foot of a towering mountainside to escape all the attention. It was strikingly beautiful terrain. The house was right down the road from the High Hampton Inn, a great rambling edifice noteworthy for years throughout the South for its gracious lobby and vast dining room, family-oriented hospitality, and being the former estate of the Confederate General Wade Hampton. The Inn was packed with families from all over Dixie the night we dined there.

We were having drinks in the bar with the owner of the High Hampton, who told us a gentleman staying in the Inn and pretending to be Winston Groom had for the last three or four days been signing copies of *Forrest Gump*. He was a good fellow, too, the owner said. The word had gotten out in the Inn and the neighborhood that the author of *Forrest Gump* was vacationing in the area, and somehow everyone thought this man was Winston Groom. In a little while, by merest coincidence, the imposter himself entered the bar, and our host introduced him to the real author. The jovial pretender was from a small town in Alabama, at least six inches shorter than the authentic Groom, yet with a vague facial resemblance. He explained he had been sitting at the bar the other night when a woman approached him. "Mr. Groom," she asked, "will you sign my book?" "I'm not Mr. Groom," he replied. "Oh, yes you are." It was easier to sign the book than not, he said, and that was the genesis of it. People were flocking to him. "I hope you don't mind," he said to Winston.

"To the contrary, I appreciate it," Winston said. "You're doing my work for me." Even as they stood there and amiably chatted, a matronly woman stepped forward and asked the interloper to sign a book, and he graciously did so. Later, at dinner upstairs, he was three or four tables away, where we noticed him signing more books for other guests. In the lobby after dinner, I sighted him again, left my companions, and asked him if he would sign my book. "I'm through autographing for the night," he said. "Try me tomorrow."

As we were walking back to his house in the invigorating mountain night, Winston said: "Life's a box of chocolates, Morris. You never know what you're gonna get."

A Long-ago Rendezvous
with Alger Hiss

(Editor's note: Alger Hiss died on November 15, 1996. This previously unpublished essay is from Willie Morris's personal files.)

I saw on CNN tonight that Alger Hiss had died at age ninety-two. In a funny way it saddened me. I remembered Mr. Hiss quite vividly.

It was 1970 and I was a magazine editor in New York City. An acquaintance of mine who worked for national educational television was a neighbor of Alger Hiss's in Greenwich Village and asked me to have dinner with them one evening. When we arrived at the tiny darkened Italian restaurant on one of those meandering, directionless smaller streets of the Village, Alger Hiss was already there, at a table with a checkered tablecloth in a corner.

He was a tall, handsome man in his late sixties wearing a lightweight summer suit and striped Ivy League tie. Somehow I had thought he might be furtive and uneasy, this enigmatic figure whose case before the House Un-American Activities Committee in 1948 had been Richard Nixon's ticket to national prominence, and I half expected him in the faint, flickering candlelight to glance about the room for incipient eavesdroppers. But all the waiters knew him—"How are you, Mr. Hiss?" "How's business, Mr. Hiss?"—and he was so relaxed and congenial, with gestures at once energetic yet casual, that I realized I was the nervous one.

This man, who had once been a protégé of Supreme Court justices Oliver Wendell Holmes, Jr., and Felix Frankfurter, attended the Yalta Conference as one of President Franklin D. Roosevelt's advisors. For a time he served as Secretary-General of the United Nations during its formative meetings in San Francisco in 1945. He had been out of federal prison since 1954, where he had served almost four years for perjury for denying he was a Soviet spy. When he emerged from prison, he had found his legal career and his marriage at an end, the U.S. Supreme Court having refused to hear his case, and he now worked as a stationery salesman.

His manner was patrician and intellectual, leavened with an avid curiosity about many topics. He wanted to know where my magazine, *Harper's*, was printed, and did they also do our stationery, or could he? When I told him our printers in Garden City ran *Mad* magazine off the presses just before ours every month and that the fellows who worked the presses played a trick on me one day when I was out there since I always loved to watch presses at work, their handing me the first copy of my magazine which happened to be a combination of our pages and *Mad*'s, he laughed and said, "An illustrious blend—half *Harper's*, half *Mad*." He had known two or three of the *Harper's* editors in the thirties, he said, and wanted to know if they were still there.

We talked for a time about this older New York and then about Oliver Wendell Holmes. From my reading I recalled to him about the day Abraham Lincoln came to the outskirts of Washington to inspect the Federal entrenchments. He stood there in his stovepipe hat as Confederate bullets whipped all around, and Captain Holmes wrestled him down and warned, "Be careful, you fool!" Hiss said, "Holmes was one of the greatest men I ever knew."

He recommended the lasagna in this comradely establishment, and while we dined, we discussed at considerable length his sister Anna Hiss, who was the director of women's physical education at the University of Texas during my days there. She was a capable and domineering figure from my recollection of her. I longed to tell him that when a bright young reporter for the intrepid *Daily Texan* came to me when I was its editor proposing a story on Anna Hiss as the sister of the traitor Alger Hiss, I had discouraged it on the grounds that it was not she who had been involved in such malfeasances.

I longed, out of old reportorial instincts on that pleasant yet vaguely discomfiting evening in that Village trattoria, to ask him if Whitaker Chambers really had such bad teeth, as everyone said he did, and if

Chambers had really hidden in a pumpkin the microfilm he said Hiss had given him, and what had really happened to the mysterious missing Ford convertible, and had he really, as an amateur ornithologist, spotted the prothonotary warbler as Chambers had reported, and what was it really like being a villainous celebrity in the very palpitating heart of this town? In my deepest being, in fact, I yearned suddenly to inquire: "Mr. Hiss, did you *do* it, or did you *not* do it?" On a social evening of pasta and Chianti even in that elusive faubourg, the quintessential things are often left unsaid.

After dinner, as he rose to leave, reaching on a nearby hat rack for a modish straw hat, we shook hands and promised to meet again. I watched a little sadly as the proud, unconfessing aristocratic old stationery salesman waved farewell to the waiters and disappeared into the warm summer vibrance of Sullivan Street, just another New York circumstance. I never saw him again.

Mississippi Queen

The night sky over my childhood Jackson was velvety black. I could see the full constellations in it and call their names; when I could read, I knew their myths. Though I was always waked for eclipses, and indeed carried to the window as an infant in arms and shown Halley's Comet in my sleep, and though I'd been taught at our dining room table about the solar system and knew the earth revolved around the sun, and our moon around us, I never found out the moon didn't come up in the west until I was a writer and Herschel Brickell, the literary critic, told me after I misplaced it in a story. He said valuable words to me about my new profession: "Always be sure you get your moon in the right part of the sky."

— Eudora Welty, *One Writer's Beginnings*

One recent Sunday I drove Eudora Welty along the spooky, kudzu-enveloped dirt and gravel back roads of Yazoo County, Mississippi, some forty miles north of Jackson. Dwarfed like a child by the stark bluffs outside the car window, she rode shotgun through the sunlight and misty shadows. "I haven't even seen another car yet," she noted at one point. "When *was* the last time we saw a human being?" Her voice, according to her friend the novelist Reynolds Price, remains "shy, but reliable as any iron beam."

She was game for anything, always peering around the next bend. At the crest of a bosky hill, a narrower and darker byway intersected with the one on which we were traveling. "Eudora, I'm going to make a left and drive down Paradise Road," I said. "We'd be fools if we didn't," she replied.

One of Eudora Welty's fictional characters had occasion to remark that against old mortality life "is nothing but the continuity of its love." Welty, often called the Jane Austen of American letters, has charted this continuity in thirteen books, including: three novels (*The Optimist's Daughter*, published in 1972, won the Pulitzer Prize); five collections of short stories; two novellas; a volume of essays; an acclaimed memoir, *One Writer's Beginnings;* and a children's book. (She has also published two volumes of her photographs, taken in Mississippi and elsewhere.)

Her work, marked by what the critic Jonathan Yardley calls an "abiding tolerance . . . a refusal to pass judgment on the actors in the human comedy," has won every literary prize except the Nobel, for which she has frequently been mentioned. Says Price, "In all of American fiction, she stands for me with only her peers—Melville, James, Hemingway, and Faulkner—and among them she is, in some crucial respects, the most life-giving." She once wrote, "My wish, indeed my continuing passion, would be not to point the finger in judgment, but to part a curtain, that invisible shadow that falls between people; the veil of indifference to each other's presence, each other's wonder, each other's human plight."

Eudora Welty, whom many consider America's greatest living writer, was born in Jackson ninety years ago. On April 13 she enters her ninety-first year. She is abidingly revered in her hometown, where her birthdays are cause for celebration. In 1994, when Eudora and friends gathered at her favorite restaurant, Bill's Tavern (which she helped get started by supplying quotes of praise for the newspaper), a Greek belly dancer performed. Above her navel were written the words "Eudora Welty I love you." During another celebration, at Lemuria Bookstore, letters were read from comrades and admirers around the world, including President Clinton. John Ferrone, her Harcourt Brace editor, wrote:

> *Hail Eudora*
> *Staunch perennial*
> *I'm looking forward*
> *to your centennial*

Eudora, who is quite simply the funniest person I have ever known, could easily have become the grande dame of American letters, but clearly would have found herself tittering at such a self-important posture. She is wryly self-effacing with a gentle irony. Our connections go back considerably, for I was born in a house two blocks from hers in the Bellhaven neighborhood of Jackson and christened in the church of her childhood, Galloway Memorial Methodist, where as a girl she took nickels to Sunday school in her glove. I met her when I was eight or nine and can pinpoint exactly where: Eudora always shopped for groceries at an erstwhile establishment called the Jitney Jungle, which had wooden floors and flypaper dangling from the ceiling. One afternoon during World War II, on one of my many sojourns into Jackson from my home in Yazoo City, I accompanied my great-aunt Maggie, who was wearing a flowing black dress, to fetch a head of lettuce, or a muskmelon perhaps. Eudora was at the vegetable counter when my great-aunt introduced us. I remember her as tall and slender, her eyes luminous blue. As we were leaving, my great-aunt whispered, "She writes those stories *her own self.*"

Through the years I have learned to expect certain kinds of reactions from Eudora. For example, when one telephones her for a meeting, she does not say, "Let's have lunch," but rather, "We *must* meet." Her conversation is laced with phrases such as "That smote me," and with solicitous interrogations, including "Don't you think?" or "Can't you imagine?" Josephine Haxton of Jackson, who writes under the nom de plume Ellen Douglas, first met her many years ago when Eudora went to Greenville, Mississippi, to sign copies of a book called *Music from Spain.* "Many years later, when my children were long since grown and had children of their own," Josephine tells me, "Eudora said to me, 'Oh, I remember so well that day I came to Greenville to sign books. Your children—those *beautiful* children.' " Others recall such instances of her magnanimous spirit. One of them, the historian and novelist Shelby Foote, tells me, "In Eudora's case, familiarity breeds affection."

Stories about her have always abounded in Jackson. In the 1930s there was not much to do in town and she and her comrades had to look hard for entertainment. They were especially intrigued when one Jackson lady announced in the paper that her night-blooming cereus was about to blossom. According to Eudora's friend Suzanne Marrs, "Eudora and her group would often gather to attend the bloomings, and they eventually formed the Night-Blooming Cereus Club, of which Eudora was elected president. Their motto was: 'Don't take it cereus; life's too mysterious.' "

Patti Carr Black, recently retired as director of the Mississippi State Historical Museum, is one of the best sources of Welty anecdotes. "My favorite hours," she says, "are spent with Eudora in the late afternoon sipping Powers Irish Whiskey and going back in her incredible memory to high times in our favorite spot, New York City. She quotes entire Bea Lillie lyrics, especially 'It's Better with Your Shoes Off'; delivers Bert Lahr punch lines; and describes the moves of the Marx Brothers and W. C. Fields, including Fields's wiggle of his little finger. She also does a great rendition of Mae West inspecting the troops up and down."

But it isn't just the locals who savor their memories of Eudora. William Maxwell, who was her editor at *The New Yorker* beginning in 1951, loves to recall her visits to New York, particularly one specific night. "When I first got to know her she was staying in the apartment of her friend and editor at *Harper's Bazaar* Mary Louise Aswell, and what I remember of the evening is Eudora's acting out of her mother telling her niece the story of Little Red Riding Hood while simultaneously reading *Time* magazine. It could have been transferred to the stage without a single change of any kind, and I didn't know anybody could be so hilarious. Some years later, when we were living on the fifth floor of a walk-up in Murray Hill, she came with the manuscript of a novella, *The Ponder Heart,* and after coffee we settled down to hear her read it. In no time I was wiping my eyes. Nothing has ever seemed so funny since. What the world must be like for a person with so exquisite a sense of humor, I don't dare think."

At dinners these days Eudora's stories move here and there like a gentle breeze that emanates from Greenwich Village in the Prohibition years, past the names of friends long dead, and on to her travels through Mississippi with her Kodak during the Depression, when she worked as a photographer. Questions provoke peregrinations. "Eudora," I asked during a recent gathering, "would you like a little kitten? I have one named Bubba." "Well," Eudora began, "mine has been a dog house all my life. My mother can't stand the thought of a cat. Of course, she's been dead a number of years. I like little kittens, but I don't think I can take one. I remember [novelist] Caroline Gordon. The first time I ever saw her, I was living in the Village, and I was going to meet her. I was walking along Eighth Avenue and she was carrying around a bunch of newborn kittens with her, and she'd go up to people on the street and say, 'You look like a cat person. Wouldn't you like a kitten?' It didn't work very well. She had a good many left. Whatever became of those kittens, I've wondered."

No one else answers questions in quite this way now, not even in Jackson.

Eudora has never married, and she lives alone in the house her father built in 1925 when she was sixteen and the nearby streets were gravel and there were whispery pine forests all around. On the front lawn is a majestic oak tree. ("Never cut an oak," her mother advised her.) The kitchen of the old house looks out on a deep-green garden with its formal bench beneath another towering oak tree. Eudora loves what she still calls "my mother's garden" and says she was "my mother's yard boy."

Her Tudor-style house has a sturdy vestibule, a brown gabled roof on the second story, and a screened-in side porch long unused. Excluding the time she has spent traveling, she has lived and worked here for seventy-four years. "I like being in the house where nobody else has ever lived but my own family," she says, "even though it's lonely being the only person left."

She calls it "my unruly home." Books of all kinds are everywhere, stacked in corners, on tables and chairs. There are mountains of books, and on every flat surface one finds unanswered mail. Her correspondence is so voluminous, she says, that she is unable to handle it. In a box on a table is the Richard Wright Medal for Literary Excellence she received in 1994. "I'm proud to have it," she says.

These days Eudora does not dress up for visitors. On the morning of one of my calls she was wearing a blue sweat suit and white sneakers. Her short hair curls around the top of her ears. Her eyes are large, very blue, a little sad, yet still, at times, vibrant with mischief. She sits near a front window in an electric lift chair that makes it easy for her to stand up. She calls it her "ejection seat." If it is late afternoon and she feels up to it, she will press the button to raise herself to an upright position and suggest you join her in the pantry while she pours a couple of Maker's Marks. "This is what Katherine Anne Porter called 'swish likka,' " she says, quoting "swich licour" from Chaucer. "This is powerful stuff." Then, faithfully at six P.M., she turns on the television for her favorite program, *The NewsHour with Jim Lehrer*.

Every conversation is a procession of supple images.

One day after a winter storm in Jackson—the first real one here in years—she recalled for her friend Hunter Cole the first time she saw snow, from her elementary-school windows on North Congress Street. It was not cold enough for it to stick, she recalled, so the teacher raised a window, took off her cape, and extended it outside. Then the woman walked hurriedly about the classroom with the garment, showing the young writer and her contemporaries the glistening snowflakes.

She is not, by birth, what is called here "Old Jackson." Her father, a northerner originally from Ohio, was the top man in a fledgling insurance company. Her southern mother had been born in West Virginia. "I was always aware," Eudora has written, "that there were two sides to most questions." Before they built the house in Belhaven the Weltys lived on North Congress Street, right down from her elementary school. (The writer Richard Ford later grew up directly across from the old Welty house.) The family was by no means rich but lived comfortably, and Eudora's parents were particularly attentive to her. In *One Writer's Beginnings*, Eudora wrote of mornings in the household of her childhood. "When I was young enough to still spend a long time buttoning my shoes in the morning," she began, "I'd listen toward the hall: Daddy upstairs was shaving in the bathroom and Mother downstairs was frying the bacon. They would begin whistling back and forth to each other up and down the stairwell. My father would whistle his phrase, my mother would try to whistle, then hum hers back. It was their duet. I drew my buttonhook in and out and listened to it—I knew it was 'The Merry Widow.' The difference was, their song almost floated with laughter: how different from the record, which growled from the beginning, as if the Victrola were only slowly being wound up."

Her father, Christian Webb Welty, had "an almost childlike love of the ingenious." Eudora believes he owned the first Dictaphone in town and he put the earphones over her ears to let her discover what she could hear. He also owned one of the early automobiles, in which the family made long journeys on perilous gravel roads to Ohio and West Virginia. Her father told Eudora and her two younger brothers, Walter and Edward, that if they were ever lost in a strange land to look for where the sky is brightest along the horizon. "That reflects the nearest river. Strike out for a river and you will find habitation." This helped provide her with what she terms "a strong meteorological sensibility." As for her mother, Chestina Welty, "valiance was in her very fibre."

The Weltys loved literature. They had an encyclopedia in the dining room, and if someone had a question at the table, someone else was always jumping up to prove the other right or wrong. As a girl, Eudora's mother had been given a complete set of Charles Dickens's novels as a reward for having her hair cut, and when the Welty home caught fire one night before Eudora was born, Mrs. Welty—on crutches at the time—returned to the house and threw all twenty-four volumes one by one out the window for Mr. Welty to catch.

It was a disappointment to the young Eudora to discover that storybooks had been written by people, "that books were not natural wonders, coming up of themselves like grass." She was in love with books, their words, their smell, their covers and bindings. The public library was on the other side of the state capitol from her home, and on her trips to get books she would glide along the marble floors of the capitol on roller skates. This produced "very desirable echoes."

At the library itself, Mrs. Calloway, a witchlike lady with a dragon eye, intimidated the children. But she could not inhibit Eudora's reading, for her mother had told the librarian: "Eudora is nine years old and has my permission to read any book she wants from the shelves, children or adult, with the exception of *Elsie Dinsmore*."

She was absorbed by the stories all around her, the eternal and ubiquitous Mississippi storytelling she heard from family, neighbors, maids. Preparing for a Sunday-afternoon ride, she would settle onto the backseat between her mother and a friend and command, "Now talk!"

At the time, Jackson girls took piano lessons as a matter of course. Eudora's own teacher, "Old Jackson" to the core, dipped her pen in ink and wrote "Practice!" on her sheet music with a *P* that resembled a cat's face with a long tail, and slapped her fingers with a flyswatter when she made a mistake.

Even as a child she was drawn to the bizarre, the grotesque, the phantasmagoric. "This being the state capital, we had all the state institutions in Jackson—blind, deaf and dumb, insane," she once observed to me. "Made for good characters." There was also the occasional society murder, which Eudora found singularly fascinating. She recalls the Mississippi matron whom I myself had heard about who was convicted for the murder of her mother; part of the corpse was found, but not all of it. She was sent to Whitfield, the asylum. Eudora and all of us heard the stories of the bridge games the murderess played with other proper ladies confined there for alcoholism. One afternoon one of the ladies abruptly tossed down her bridge hand and said, "Not another card will I play until you tell me what you did with the rest of your mother."

In Eudora's childhood years, the two Jackson newspapers published the honor rolls and individual grades of all the honor students. Also, the city fathers gave the honor children free season tickets to the baseball games of the noble Jackson Senators of the Class B Cotton States League. Eudora adored Red McDermott, the Senators' third-baseman, and offered him her documents attesting to her 100s in all her subjects, even attendance and deportment. At age twelve she won the Jackie Mackie Jingle contest, sponsored by the Mackie Pine Oil Company of Covington, Louisiana; the company president sent her a $25 check and said he hoped she would "improve American poetry to such an extent as to win fame."

Eudora spent two years in the little town of Columbus, Mississippi—Tennessee Williams's birthplace—at the Mississippi State College for Women. Although "the W," as it is called, was impoverished, neglected, and overcrowded, Eudora remembers it as a place of great intellectual stimulation, with a dedicated cadre of female teachers who taught without pay for months during the Depression when the state could not pay their salaries. The college brought together 1,200 girls from every corner of Mississippi. They all wore identical uniforms, but Eudora learned to tell where a girl had grown up from the way she talked, ate, or entered a classroom. She once told me that she could distinguish a girl from the Delta by the way she walked.

Eudora became a cartoonist for the school paper and was chosen fire chief of Hastings Hall. At night she frequently sneaked out of the dorm to go downtown, where the action was, and, on one such evening, won a Charleston contest at the Princess Theater. Elizabeth Spencer first met Eudora some years after this when the former was a college student. "I was in great awe of her talent," Elizabeth remembers, "but I was not aware of her high-flying sense of humor." Then one afternoon the two of them were at a post office and noticed a tacked-up poster proclaiming:

NO LOITERING OR SOLICITING. "Eudora saw it," Elizabeth recalls, "and said, 'Let's loiter and solicit.'" When Elizabeth said O.K., Eudora declared, "Then you solicit while I loiter."

Eudora's father, the northerner, wanted his daughter to spend her last two college years at some distinguished university up North, and in 1927 she enrolled at the University of Wisconsin. Her mother was already encouraging her aspirations to become a writer, and Mr. Welty gave his daughter her first typewriter, a little red Royal Portable, which she took with her to Madison. To get her through the harsh winters he also bought her a possum coat at Marshall Field in Chicago. Many of the students, she recalls, had raccoon coats, but her family could not afford such luxury.

At first, the Midwest frightened her. Years later she wrote her longtime agent, Diarmuid Russell, about her first months above the Mason-Dixon line: "I was very timid and shy, younger than the rest and those people up there seemed to me like sticks of flint that live in the icy world. I am afraid of flintiness—I had to penetrate that. . . . I used to be in a kind of wandering daze, I would wander down to Chicago and through the stores, I could feel such a heavy heart inside me. It was more than the pangs of growing up, much more. It was some kind of desire to be shown that the human spirit was not like that shivery winter in Wisconsin, that the opposite to all this existed in full."

Her father, concerned about his daughter's future, persuaded her to go to graduate school in business. She immediately chose Columbia University because she wanted to live in New York for a year. She studied typing for a while, "so I could be a secretary and make a living." When she had to pick a major subject she selected advertising, "which wasn't awfully good, because all at once, when the Depression hit, nobody had any money to advertise with. For that matter, nobody had any money to do anything with." During the Manhattan winter her mother sent her boxes of camellias to remind her of home.

In 1931, shortly after Eudora returned to Jackson from New York City, her father died of leukemia. Her mother was left with two sons in high school and college, so Eudora worked at whatever she could do. Her first job, at age twenty-two, was at a local radio station headquartered in the clock tower of Jackson's first skyscraper: the Lamar Life building, which had been built by her father's company.

As part of her job she wrote the radio schedule to mail out to listeners and also sent fake letters to the station which were to be read on the air: "Dear WJDX, I love the opera on Saturday. Don't ever take it away!" She remembered the office as being "as big as a chicken coop," with just enough room for Mr. Wiley Harris, the announcer and manager, and herself. He would go up into the clock tower to clean out the canary's cage, and she would yell "Mr. Harris! Mr. Harris!" because it was time for him to announce the call letters of the station. The absentminded Mr. Harris would come down and say, "This is Station . . . uh, this . . . This is Station . . ." Eudora would write the call letters—WJDX—on a sheet of cardboard and hold it up for him.

Later, still during the Depression, she was hired as a publicity agent, junior grade, with the Works Progress Administration. She visited the farm-to-market roads in Mississippi and interviewed people living along them. She rode around on bookmobile routes and helped put up booths at county fairs. She visited landing fields being hacked out of cow pastures, juvenile courts, the scene of the devastating Tupelo tornado, and even a project teaching Braille to the blind. She went mostly by bus and stayed in the old small-town hotels. At night, under a squeaky electric fan, she wrote up the projects for the county weeklies. The Depression, she would remember, "was not a noticeable phenomenon in the poorest state in the Union."

For her own gratification, she began taking photographs, using an old-fashioned Kodak. The Standard Photo Company of Jackson developed her film, and she printed it at night in her kitchen at home. She says that her years of "snapshooting," as she calls it, helped her arrive at the perception that she must go beyond silent images to the slower voice of words.

"Mostly I remember things vividly," she says of the years she spent taking pictures. "I remember how people looked, just people standing against the sky sometimes, at the end of a day's work. Something like that is indelible to me. In taking all these pictures, I was attended, I know now, by an angel—a presence of trust. . . . It is a trust that dates the pictures, more than the vanished years."

Soon her stories started to come to her. Her very first, in 1936, was "Death of a Traveling Salesman," published in an obscure Ohio quarterly called *Manuscript*. When she was awarded a Guggenheim fellowship in 1942, she told a friend's aunt in Jackson her news. The aunt responded, "A Guggenheim what?" "I think she thought it was a hat," Eudora said.

By 1944 she had published *A Curtain of Green* and *The Robber Bridegroom*, and for six months of that year she lived again in New York City. Robert Van Gelder of *The New York Times Book Review* had interviewed her in 1942 and later offered her a job. "Can you imagine?" she remembers. "Of course, I immediately accepted and then phoned my mother in Mississippi. She was glad I'd found a job, because they weren't easy to come by during the war." But she was not entirely comfortable. "I didn't want to give a book a bad review. No matter what it is, it's a year out of somebody's life." She used the pseudonym of Michael Ravenna when reviewing war books, and when readers wrote to Michael Ravenna, she replied that he was away at the front line.

Always unabashedly stagestruck, Eudora could look outside her office window and see the performers she most admired arriving at rehearsals and performances. Mae West was rehearsing *Catherine Was Great* just next door and Eudora often slipped in the back to watch. "I'd watch during my lunch hour. Nobody seemed to mind. And I was in heaven."

In 1949, with a $5,000 advance on a new book and a second Guggenheim, she made her first trip to Europe and fell in love with Ireland, as southerners often do. She walked alone on its country roads and hid under hedges when it rained. One of her writing idols was Elizabeth Bowen, whom she visited in County Cork. Later, at Cambridge, she lunched with one of her own admirers, E. M. Forster, and became one of the few women to enter the hall of Peterhouse College. Eudora recalls, "They were so dear the way they told me: they said, 'Miss Welty, you are invited to come to this, but we must tell you that we debated for a long time about whether or not we should ask you.'"

Years later Eudora—with twenty-nine other women, including Helen Hayes, Lauren Bacall, and Toni Morrison—was invited to become a member of the Players Club on Gramercy Park, the prestigious establishment for theater people. They were the first female members. "Let's invade them, girls," Eudora announced to the assembled companions at cocktail hour.

By 1955 she had published four short-story collections, a novel, and two novellas. For the next fifteen years, with the exception of three short stories in 1963, 1966, and 1969, until the novel *Losing Battles*, there was silence. She was virtually unpublished. These were difficult years personally. Her mother had serious eye surgery, and as her complaints multiplied, her condition gradually deteriorated. Eudora had to take care of her; there were no others to do this except salaried outsiders. Eudora's brother Walter, six years younger than she, also became very ill at the age of forty with heart problems compounded by arthritis. "I'm so ashamed of not producing anything," Eudora wrote Diarmuid Russell. "I should think all of my friends would have given me up."

Walter died in 1959. Eventually, Eudora was forced to put her mother in a nursing home in Yazoo City, nearly fifty miles away. Eudora drove there and back every day of the week for more than a year to read to her and help look after her. On the long drives she sometimes made notes for *Losing Battles* in a notebook propped on the steering wheel. Her mother and her other brother, Edward, died four days apart in 1966.

To help pay for the nursing home, Eudora had to take a job teaching a writing workshop at Millsaps College in Jackson. She had sixteen talented students screened by the English Department. When the now famous writer called the roll for the first time, the students realized she was more nervous than they were. "We hadn't expected that," says John Little, who was one of the students and later became director of the writing program at the University of North Dakota. "We didn't know this was the first college class she ever taught. We didn't know she was intensely shy." After the roll call, she read Dylan Thomas's "A Child's Christmas in Wales." After the story, the students sat in stone silence. Eudora looked at her watch; they looked at theirs. Finally, Tom Royals—now a lawyer in Jackson—rescued the day. "Miss Welty," he said, "since this is the first class, we don't have to stay the whole two hours." Her sigh of relief was audible.

After a few classes they tried a more casual setting—a Sunday-night social at someone's house. John Little got there late; he was carrying a case of cold Budweiser on his shoulder. The hostess frowned at the beer and sent the young man to the kitchen with it. The stifling silence from the living room matched that of the classroom. "Anybody want a Bud?" Little shouted. "Please," came one small voice from the silence. It was

Eudora's. "The sight of Miss Welty drinking that beer had the sound of ice breaking," Little says.

Eudora's closest friend, in almost every way a sister, was Charlotte Capers, who died two years ago at age eighty-three. Charlotte, author of an essay collection entitled *The Capers Papers,* and a friend of my own family's, was a descendant of Episcopal bishops and Sewanee College presidents, and one of the brightest, wackiest women on earth. To each other they were "Cha-Cha," pronounced with a soft *ch,* and "Dodo," like the note. Once not long before her death when she and another companion were helping Eudora into a four-door sedan, Capers said, "Let's get Dodo . . . into the fo'do'."

Up until fairly recently, Eudora drove an ancient Oldsmobile Cutlass, and the sight of her, barely able to see over the steering wheel, making her way to Parkin's Pharmacy to buy *The New York Times,* was as familiar as another picture we all have in our memories, Eudora's profile through the open windows of her second floor, as she sat at her writing desk. She always declared that her work made her happy and fulfilled. With short stories she always tried to get down a first draft spontaneously, often in a single day's work. "After that," she says, "I revised with scissors and pins. Pasting is too slow and you can't undo it, but with pins you can move things from anywhere to anywhere, and that's what I really love doing—putting things in their best and proper place, revealing things at the time when they matter most. Often I shift things from the very beginning to the very end. Small things—one fact, one word—but things important to me. It's possible I have a reverse mind, and do things backwards, being a broken left-hander."

Because of her health, Eudora has a hard time writing now. "My body doesn't help me anymore," she tells me, quoting a friend.

Eudora was a tall woman in her prime, but osteoporosis and a compression fracture in her back eight years ago have left their mark. She has arthritis in her hands and can no longer use a typewriter. Some years ago, the New Stage, a community theater group in Jackson, had a rummage sale. Eudora drove over in her old car and took a half-dozen hand-blown Czechoslovak Easter eggs and an old Royal typewriter in its original travel case. It was the typewriter her father had given her years before, the typewriter on which she had written her novels and stories since the 1930s. Jack Stevens, an actor, bought it for $10. Later he donated it to the State Archives.

She laments not having direct access to the written page as she once did, in the days when we all watched her working as we walked or drove past the house. Directly across the street from the Welty home was the music building of Belhaven College, and from the practice rooms the sounds of piano music would drift across Pinehurst Street, keeping her company through the long and solitary hours at the old Royal. "Though I was as constant in my work as the students were," she has written, "subconsciously I must have been listening to them, following them. . . . I realized that each practice session reached me as an outpouring. And those longings, so expressed, so insistent, called up my longings unexpressed. I began to hear, in what kept coming across the street into the room where I typed, the recurring dreams of youth, inescapable, never to be renounced, naming themselves over and over again."

The South and
Welcome to It:
Does It Still Exist?

The Round-Up

FEBRUARY 23, 1955

It is strange, somehow, but inexorably shaped and nurtured within us—we Americans, I mean—the steadfast and earnest inner-voice which ever calls us to the places of our upbringing.

Perhaps this is meant to be, this sanguine, inwrought magnetism of home. Perhaps, born of the loneliness which we feel so pungently on the vast continent of America, in its teeming city-jungles, its raw, ugly, unending countrysides, its unnumbered little towns, we are invisibly impelled to know and seek one thin portion of space where all the multiple man-elements of life-on-earth appear in clearer, cleaner, nobler focus.

I have known those who, more from this selfsame loneliness and shame than anything else, have disowned the places of their youth. Yet, even with the supercilious sneer and the acrid sarcasm upon their lips, I see, and feel, and understand, with an understanding that arises from my own deep loneliness, and the loneliness of all men. For, in the very act of their denial, they will acknowledge something rich and complete which they have left behind them—a part of their youth, their first-sights, first-sounds, first-perceptions, and later, their first-loves, first-hates, first-hopes. They dream of successes in far lands, of deeds fit only for the poet to tell, and of the inevitable return to main street, and all the "I knew him when's," wrought out of our American reverence for self-made success, which is as much a part of our land and our people as Christmas Eve and 25 cent novels and dusty Johnson grass and Sunday doubleheaders.

Just as all men, I have come to know this inner-link with home, for it is a part of me, forged into my blood, and there forever.

And this is the way it came about, and this is the way it affects me:

As a small boy, standing at the brink of the intersection of the main street of my home city and the highway—one of those gushing national arteries that pushes people along with an intensity known only to the frequent traveler—I would spend a hundred drowsy summer days watching the blind stream of mighty diesels and buses and cotton trucks roll past. Once, two travelers, a man and his wife, stopped for gas at a service station near by. The woman looked about her with the suave almightiness of the well-kept Northerner. "My," she said to her companion, "what an ugly little town."

As I grew older, and left this ugly little city, and tried, in scholarly compliance to the affectations of society, to become academic and urban and well-kept, a voice came to me telling of all the numberless ugly little towns of our land, each with its high school football team, its all-American boy, its corner drug, its bootlegger, its broad old movie house, its country club, its old families, its Rotary Club. And suddenly I felt a grand and irrevocable attachment to all of them, and I became obsessed with a glorious desire to see and know them all.

On Saturday nights in the soft summertime, with the message of the good crop on every lip, the main street in my home town is the epitome of civilization. Around the Dixie Theater the earth's rusty old axis revolves, and a thousand universes away. In the warm laughter of the Negroes—hundreds of them, escaping for four hours a week of sweat and cotton and black dirt—I hear the raw joy of all living. Ford and Chrysler are guided by the Saturday night ebb-flow of cars on main street in my hometown, all valor sighs when a rough farmer's son enlists in the Army at the post office, new formulas spring up full-born at DuPont when someone seeks an undiscovered pill at the corner drug. There is beauty in the gaunt gray courthouse, where Law, both ruthless and understanding, has prevailed; in the red-brick Elks Club, the skinny traffic light at Jefferson and Main, the Bon-Ton, the Confederate monument.

And this is why the staunch old American pull of home affects me. It is born of many things, but mostly of loneliness and love, of people known and people forgotten, of a hillside cemetery and sweet-potato pie, of a country curve and a sweaty baseball suit, of a fat old dog and a Negro maid, of the neighbors' boys and a high school enemy, of the morning paper and the evening meal, of the dance band at midnight and the urgency of noon. All the lost and dead moments of youth and going-away have become a part of me, and I a part of them.

And as I tell of these things, selfishly perhaps, I know with a firm certitude I am not alone. I know that all men feel the pulsating call of home—home to the asphalt interiors of Houston, home to the drab expanses of El Paso, home to the far-land of Detroit, home to Muleshoe, home to Marshall, homes magical, homes commonplace, homes with a million different faces in a million different corners of our land. For this is our heritage, this is our birthright, and no man, even he with the petty cynicism that comes of both fame and obscurity, can deny it.

The Round-Up

A newspaper is no schoolboy proposition.

It affects minds, and minds affect people, and people affect other people, and soon there is a sociological reaction that reaches the very nerve-ends of our politics, our education, and our literature.

R. K. Towery, homespun Cuero editor whose pluck and go won a Pulitzer prize last month, said it better. "A newspaper," he wrote, "affects the lives and decisions of many people. It is called upon to state views that some would rather not hear. It is called upon to support a cause that some would rather not support, and it is called upon in time of crises to choose between one side or another."

We accept the editorship of this, the greatest of all college newspapers, with a confidence and faith—not in ourselves, for that would be blind egotism—but in the men and women of this University. Every word we print, utter, or delete is directed toward their better interests.

There will be times we'll misunderstand one another. There will be wandering tempers, bitter words, and whispered threats. There will be polite threats, which is worse. But always, we trust, there will be the gradual uneven flow of progress, the improvement in mind and matter that is absolutely essential to civilization as we know it.

Perhaps, when we see ourselves alienated in principle or in fact, we can meet on common ground—that of honest, unrestricted discussion. The *Texan* office is always open. Drop by at any time to kibitz or to present your peeves.

What about the editor? You have a right to know something about the man who will provoke sneers and censures and perhaps a few smiles during the next twelve months.

Most important, he is a strong believer in a free, unhindered press.

The Yankees threw his great-grandfather's presses in the town well in 1863, and he hasn't forgotten it.

Politically, he is uncommitted. With great disgust he has seen the American party system evolve into one prodigious Overlapping. The only partisan label he applies is one of an independent seeker and reporter of the truth.

He is a liberal if liberalism means open-mindedness, fairness, and support of change when change is needed.

He thinks there should exist a certain innate detachment, call it hostility if you will, between a newspaper and a community's elected and administrative officials. Joseph Pulitzer once said a newspaper had no friends. To rephrase, the *Texan* has no obligations.

He believes 1955 is a crossroads year for this institution.

With enrollment figures due to multiply enormously, he will settle only for the most judicious planning on both administrative and student levels.

For examples of truly great *Daily Texans,* he looks to those published by Bob Owens, by Horace Busby, and by Ronnie Dugger.

As for promises, he will commit himself to one: Should *The Daily Texan* ever become intolerant, illiberal, dependent, apologetic, fawning, or the megaphone of any man or group of men, he will resign without hearing.

"If the people care for a fair, hard-hitting paper that will stand for the best in the community," wrote William Allan White, "here it is."

Here we are, and we invite you to join us.

Mississippi Rebel on
a Texas Campus

About the Author: The fight for press freedom waged by William W. Morris,
editor of the Daily Texan, *campus daily of the University of Texas, has been*
front-page news for weeks. Mr. Morris is one of the university's outstanding
students, a Phi Beta Kappa and winner of a Rhodes Scholarship (he goes to
Oxford in October). He is also a Southerner born and bred. He writes: "I spent
the first seventeen years of my life in Yazoo City, Mississippi, ninety miles
south of Hodding Carter's Greenville, 120 miles south of William Faulkner's
Oxford, and forty miles north of Eudora Welty's Jackson."

AUSTIN, TEXAS—The current controversy between my newspaper, the
Daily Texan, and the University of Texas Board of Regents goes much
deeper than one might believe. This newspaper has always been one of
the nation's finest college dailies; its editorial prerogative has always been
something to be admired; and in times of stress for the university it
has risen to heights that would do credit to the mature profession. The
controversy transcends the locale. It represents a typical intrusion of state
politics into education. It underscores the coercion exercised by economic
interests whose endeavors to mold conformity and stifle dissent are rather
prominent in our country today. And it calls attention to one of the less
noble of our American traditions: the tradition of a "kept" college press,
badgered by state legislatures, college administrators, and students themselves, and all but ignored by professional journalism.

It was six weeks ago that the university regents, appointees of Governor Allan Shivers, announced they were tightening up on *Daily Texan*
editorial policy. Obviously they had been highly disturbed by certain
aspects of the *Texan's* categorical defense of student press freedom and

its editorial comments on "controversial" state and national issues. The *Texan* had gone on record against the Shivers administration. It had deplored scandals which had rocked Texas in past months. It had asked that the state's oil and gas interests pay more taxes. It had sought intelligence, good will, and enlightened gradualism in the university's desegregation problem, and had lauded Texans for their moderate but tolerant approach to integration. It had stood firmly against the Harris-Fulbright natural-gas bill, one of the few Texas papers to do so. In short, it had committed the crime of being vigorous and outspoken, naively idealistic and exuberantly but not radically liberal in a predominantly conservative state.

Many times previously members of the board of regents had shown their disapproval of the paper's policies. Prior to the executive session in which they unanimously drafted the censorship edict, they advertised—perhaps far more than they intended—their political and economic allegiances. At an official meeting with student body representatives, they angered some of the campus's outstanding young leaders, including the student president and vice-president, by asserting that the *Daily Texan* should not discuss controversial state and national topics, by announcing that college students were not interested in such topics, by saying that the *Texan* had gone far astray in criticizing the Harris-Fulbright bill, and by accusing the editor of being a "mouthpiece," supposedly for Texas liberals.

Describing their censorship edict as based on legal considerations rather than principle, they cited the rider on state appropriation bills, which says no state money "shall be used for influencing the outcome of any election, or the passage or defeat of any legislative measure." Advancing a step further, they announced that "editorial preoccupation with state and national political controversy" would also be prohibited.

The edict was promptly tested. Two highly critical editorials outlining the implications of the order were submitted to the editorial director and the acting dean of the School of Journalism, the regents' delegated representatives. A guest editorial from the *New York Times* attacking the Harris-Fulbright bill was also submitted, as were several paragraphs by Thomas Jefferson on press freedom, written under the guise of a personal column. All were rejected. The editor then called a meeting of the student-dominated Texas Student Publications board of directors, quasi-publishers of the *Daily Texan*. The students approved the editorials, and they were printed in the next day's paper. The controversy was underway.

In the days that followed, the *Texan* editorialized vehemently against the move to suppress. The student body, for the most part, was sympathetic. Roland Dahlin, the student president and an advocate of campus press freedom, helped organize the resistance. He authorized a brilliant young law student, William Wright, to represent the students legally. Wright, conferring with some of Texas's most respected attorneys and legal scholars, refuted the applicability of the appropriations rider by pointing up the *Texan's* financial independence (its funds are derived from two sources: student activity fees and advertising). He said the regents' interpretation of the rider had "terrifying implications" and reasoned it could be used just as logically, or illogically, to stifle legitimate comment among students, faculty, and quasi-independent corporations housed on the campus: the Ex-Students' Association, the Texas Law Review, and others.

The student legislature by a 25 to 1 vote, passed a free-press resolution. Later the Texas Intercollegiate Students' Association, representing most of the state's colleges and universities, approved a similar resolution. Campus organizations, including the Young Democrats and the Young Republicans, lined up with the *Texan*. On the other hand, the faculty—publicly at least—kept silent.

Certain regents fought back. Claude Voyles, a ranchman and oil operator, told the Austin *American*, "We feel the *Daily Texan* has gone out of bounds in discussing the Harris-Fulbright bill when 66 percent of Texas money comes from oil and gas." He also said, "We are just trying to hold [the editor] to a college yell."

J. Frank Dobie, the Texas historian and folklorist, attacked the regents: "They are as much concerned with free intellectual enterprise as a razorback sow would be with Keats's 'Ode to a Grecian Urn.'" The *Texas Observer*, a courageous liberal weekly edited by former *Texan* editor and Oxford-educated Ronnie Dugger, forged a major editorial campaign in our behalf. The New York *Post*, the St. Louis *Post-Dispatch*, the Denver *Post*, the Raleigh *News and Observer*, and the Fort Worth *Star-Telegram* editorialized favorably. But the Dallas *News*, Texas's most articulate newspaper, criticized the *Texan's* stand, as did the magazine *Editor and Publisher*. Some twenty-five college papers sided with us, two were critical. The staff of the *Texan* (Managing Editor Carl Burgen wrote, "I stand with the editor") resisted censorship; many said they would walk out if the editors were fired.

At the moment the situation is quiescent. President Logan Wilson, a capable administrator caught in the crossfire, has shuttled the issue off to the Texas Student Publications board, which recently upheld the *Daily Texan's* right to discuss state and national issues. A more substantial "re-clarification" of *Daily Texan* editorial freedoms will be prepared for the regents' consideration at their April meeting. At the moment the intentions of the board are rather dubious. There are only three journalism professors on the eleven-member body, and they are caught in the same crosscurrent. If the board does believe in student press freedom, and I am certain its members do, they nonetheless are beginning to look with much disfavor upon the individual prerogatives of an editor. There seems to be a trend toward a collectivism in thought and policy, in which the editors may be stripped of their rights on controversial topics and the board itself will frequently edit, subdue or censor. Up until now the board has officially possessed that power, but has never used it. I fear strongly that the individualism of future editors (they are elected yearly by popular vote of the student body) may be the price paid for our defiance of the regents. As the North Carolina *Daily Tar Heel*, one of the few free college papers, has editorialized: "The *Daily Texan* summoned its legal and philosophical resources and claimed uneasy victory over the regents. . . . But it was a Pyrrhic victory, almost." If the victory is Pyrrhic, it is still victory. The *Texan* is still a student newspaper, and free conscience at this university has at least won for itself a stay of execution.

The *Texan* case is nothing new to college journalism. Today the trend on American campuses is toward absolute censorship of college papers. This seems particularly true in state universities, where the power of the legislative purse string can be used to silence legitimate comment. The preponderance of censored college papers is an affront to the dignity of the nation. The "kept" ones pour into our office from all corners of the land, speaking their shameful, tongueless idiom. They hide their shame by imploring students to turn over a new leaf at the start of a semester, give blood to a blood drive, support the football team, use their leisure more wisely, collect wood for a bonfire. They are by all rights dead, victims of an educational hypocrisy worse than treason, and their meaningless editorials tear young men's guts with a frustration they cannot express.

Such seems to be the temper of the times. The First Amendment, of course, does not apply to college journalism. Institutional governing boards are autonomous, as the recent Lucy expulsion at the University of Alabama illustrates. These boards are hypersensitive to criticism from state politicians and moneyed interests. To appease legislatures, the easiest way is to suppress. Ergo, censorship; and ergo the relative few campus voices that still speak bravely. These are centered in the Ivy League, where the absolute freedom of papers like the *Harvard Crimson* and the *Cornell Sun* is taken for granted.

The current plight of college journalism can, in turn, be integrated into an even broader whole. Throughout the land, the threat to constitutional liberties is greater than ever, simply because conformity has never been so completely sanctioned economically, legally, and morally. Most American educational institutions seem to have surrendered to these official and unofficial pressures. I have lived with this stifling conformity on my own campus, and I have been frightened by it. The desire here to side with the majority has never been more manifest. One sees it everywhere: in the classroom, the coffee session, the committee meeting, the Greek lodge. The great goal at my university today is an easy and profitable job, two cars, a pretty wife, three children (two boys and a girl), two weeks' vacation with pay, and a twenty-one-inch-plus TV with at least six snow-free channels. As a consequence we are turning out accomplished nonentities, faultless and safe and more than able to please the corporation or the boss; but we are failing to turn out individuals competent and willing to test new ideas and sometimes criticize old ones. Yet it was such as these who made America.

My generation has been labeled the "silent" one, which indeed I think it is. But the generation which came before us was the lost one, until it found itself; unhappily it too has suddenly become quite silent. I am rather ashamed of our silence, and sometimes I regret we have never been lost, because we are so smugly certain of our crass goals.

nifestation of a silent age, and I have no other
the newspaper that is briefly mine against the
al, institutional and personal conformity. The
en in my fellow students' defense of press free-
on of hope. I believe that on the campuses of our
, traditional guardians of our basic liberties, must
be found ___ to the dilemma that faces the American man as
he moves closer and closer toward collective security and farther from
individual responsibility to himself, his nation, and his God.

The Rain Fell Noiselessly

YAZOO CITY, MISSISSIPPI—From Houston it was two hours in the air to Jackson. My mother was at the airport, and we drove home in the rain, forty miles to the little town built crazily here on the edge of the hills. That afternoon late I went to the hospital to see my father, then came back to our house.

There wasn't much light left and the rain was settling in for the night when Bubba came by in his pick-up and asked me to ride out and see his cotton. We drove up Washington, past the Courthouse, over the hill onto the Vicksburg highway, and there it was, the delta, spreading out before us miles and miles as far as you could see—perfectly flat, jungle green, it went on and on to the rim of the sky, ending there like a phantom in the rising grey mists. Just below the road the Yazoo River, dark, sluggish, bended and straightened and moved on toward the Mississippi, and far out to the west, far out in that alluvial flatness, there was a strip of orange, holding out stubbornly against the clouds and the night. Sometimes the sky exploded with lightning and thunder, and it rained hard.

We talked in that fashion of friends so close that long separations can never embarrass, about the things boys who grew up together in small towns, one leaving and the other staying, talk about—and always about the people who died naturally or violently or by their own hand since the last trip home. The truck rattled and groaned at each crack in the road, and we could hardly hear above the sound. But beneath the noise the mood of that moment was fragile and sad, like coming home always is. A few miles up we turned right and went through Satartia, and over the ancient river bridge to the plantation. The gravel road cut through the jungle of cotton; we were surrounded by it, and so also were the tenant houses spaced every mile or so in the fields, where it grew almost into the front yards and up onto the porches. And when I talked about Texas, about the Blakleys and Yarboroughs and Daniels and the names that made a summer, they were words and nothing more, for here they had lost their meaning and even their existence, they intruded and seemed somehow vulgar. There was only us and the truck and that unfathomable richness lurking out there in the rain. In that instant I knew the delta again.

Up the road, beyond a bend, was the house where the plantation manager lived. He was waiting on the porch. He and Bubba talked—they were getting rain on the south part, you could tell by the clouds and the lightning for sure, and the cotton looked good and they'd just have to wait now, and you could go through the rows and kill a hundred boll weevils in ten minutes with your fingers by pinching off their heads. How was the cotton further up the delta by Ruleville and Parchman and Drew? It was good, looked good everywhere, but not as good as this, probably. It might take plenty more poison pretty soon, but the best thing to do now was wait, just wait and see. . . .

Standing next to the truck, I slapped at the mosquitoes and watched a lone Negro walk slowly up the road to Satartia. Inside the manager's house the TV was on. A tiny brown dog stretched out under the truck and scratched at a flea. Far away there was the sound of a cowbell. If you closed your eyes and listened hard you would be drifting and lost in the middle of a million katy-dids: katy-did, katy-didn't, katy-did, katy-didn't; the uncompromising debate without a referee that went on forever. On the edge of the nearest fields the trees were dark blurred outlines, the last few survivors of the vanished beaten forest that once covered all this. Under the cotton in the mud there must have been water moccasins, and by the river a few alligators, for this is the country where they hunt them at night for fun.

It was all but dark now. I stood at the edge of the field, near the cotton taller than I, and listened to the powerful black land—it hummed and rustled and was alive. It whispered gently to itself, making strange alien sounds. The rain fell noiselessly on the growing plants, and somewhere in the darkness behind the trees the river ran. When we got back in the truck to drive into town the rain was harder, pelting the top of it. Then, just as suddenly, it stopped. The land sucked up at the moisture, then settled into sleep—lonely, sufficient, and aloof.

Despair in Mississippi;
Hope in Texas

I

I have been wondering recently why it was that the full barbarism of the University of Mississippi crisis did not strike me until almost three months after Meredith had been enrolled. I bought a newspaper one afternoon in San Francisco and read the wire service account of how a hundred or more students had surrounded Meredith's table in the school cafeteria. Shaking their fists, quivering like young mammals in heat, they had chanted: "Go home nigger. We don't want you here." Up to then I had read most of the reports on the demonstrations, and as editor of a small Texas journal had published a number of stories on the riots and the killing. That afternoon, I think, my final awareness of the indescribable shame had a great deal to do with the simple fact of physical *removal* from the South, where I have spent most of my life; two thousand miles away, my response was untempered by the strange compromises your emotions make, almost as a matter of course, when you are there. It was like looking at a particularly stark painting: the image of the Negro surrounded, enclosed, had no modifying details, no relief, no irony or sympathy for anyone but the victim, all the power concentrated, congealed, in his lonely anguish.

His tormentors, the chanting mob, were, I know, sons and scions of good white Mississippi families who somehow manage to invoke at every crisis, in a sort of unlettered liturgical way, the honor and pride and dignity of the Southern tradition. There sat Meredith, and there he no doubt still sits; one can only imagine how he, as a human being, must have been torn inside. Perhaps his stoic patience has, in some small measure, impinged on the honor and pride and dignity which his antagonists claim as their birthright; but for the Mississippi I know that is hoping too much.

I write about Mississippi with an almost total despair. I was born and raised there, and like most Southerners who leave home and yet come to understand, as the historian Vann Woodward says, that to throw away your Southern background for the usual brittle Americanism is affirming more than you bargain for, I feel hopelessly rooted to it, drawn back to it, not merely as an American is drawn to home, but as one is drawn to a condition of the senses, to some fragile certitude of old grief and sorrow and love. This is an unfurbished romanticism, but there is no call for either denying it, as with some exiles from the South or, as with others, exaggerating it into a lusty mystique, and making a lot of Yankee dollars in the doing. With me it is a simple fact of sensibility, and there is nothing I can do about it. Yet there is a futile, deepening ambivalence in the white Southerner's act of removal. Travelling America, he can see, all around him, what the country has become—the dream gone berserk; bleak, hollow, and homogenized. In California there is an avenue, El Camino, from Los Angeles to San Francisco, miles on end of chrome, asphalt horror, the thing we have reached, the end of the land. I remember, as a dream, Highway 49 in the Mississippi delta, superimposed almost without a curve from Yazoo City to Memphis on that black alluvial flatland. El Camino is ugly, vulgar, cheap. The delta is hot-blooded beauty, sorcery, tragedy.

One night, five or six years ago, I sat in a bar in Paris with Richard Wright. We discovered, in talking, that we had been born only a few miles apart in Mississippi. A silence fell between us, like an immense pain; or perhaps it was my imagining. For I knew that the land is bloody and full of guilt where we were born. What distinctiveness remains, in this deepest South, is rooted even yet to a life which is contradictory of civilized values. You turn on it, as it turns on Meredith, though it had turned on both of you first, years before.

The past which this South claims for you, legend though most of it is, is somehow embodied, made vivid, in those one or two or three indestructible images of your people. With me it is the great-great uncle, U.S. Senator Henry S. Foote—rascal, charlatan, courageous foe of secession and bitter enemy of Jefferson Davis (whom he once defeated for governor of Mississippi)—campaigning throughout the South against the mounting hysteria for Douglas and the Northern Democrats in 1860. It is great-grandfather George W. Harper, editor of the *Hinds County Gazette*, turning to one-mule dirt farming after the Federal troops deposited his printing press in the town well. Harper fathered sixteen children, all honorable by their own lights; only the youngest, my grandmother, remains. The last time we went to the cemetery we were unable to find a single Harper. Their graves were sunk down, overgrown, and hopelessly lost. Some yards away were the graves of a few dozen Federal troops killed in an unimportant skirmish in 1863. Their graves are well-kept—watered and flowered every year by the townspeople. You can find symbolism in this curious juxtaposition, I suppose, but the symbolism will not help you find the Harpers.

I am not quite sure what the Footes and the Harpers would have done when Governor Barnett inspired the clash at the University of Mississippi last fall. Since I assign to them neither an excess of virtue nor of evil, my guess is that, like a number of Mississippi editors, housewives, and sons of God after the murder of Emmett Till and the Battle of Ole Miss, they would have kept quiet. Yet to the vast majority of Mississippians today, even quiet is suspect. The tragedy of Mississippi is the tragedy of a society which not only does not allow dissent, but equates even silence with a kind of disloyalty. With a handful of exceptions, Mississippi is a monolith; its soul-force is its burning and ravaging and gnawing hatred. Last year, in front of a Baptist Church in Austin, Texas, there was a sentence displayed on its bulletin board: "If you want to keep a man down, you have to stay down with him." Since Mississippians have given so much of themselves to keep the Negro down, they themselves have lost some essential part of their own humanity. There is only this overriding consideration: to keep the black man down; so determined are they, so great is their fear and hatred, that even with the more sophisticated among them life is a thing of empty social ritual, intellection is shabby and false, and even in their hate there is an almost lifeless formalism. Growing up in Mississippi, you have the hatred nurtured in your bones. If it is not your parents who do the nurturing, then it is someone else; it is almost *everything* else.

For the child the moment comes early when he is forbidden to be friends with little Negroes; from that moment on he begins to sense hatred in the very atmosphere, a living, breathing, electric thing, hatred institutionalized and embodied. This is what that hatred is: As a child of seven or eight, it is sitting on the floor of a crowded room in the police station and hearing your father tell the Negro who had been caught stealing in your neighborhood, "Nigger, if you even walk down that side of the street again and I see you, I'll blow your head off with both barrels of my shotgun." It is what compels you, as a boy of nine or ten, to lurk in the shrubbery while the little Negro child walks down the sidewalk with his mother, and to jump out and knock him to the ground with your fists. It is the admonition of the white doctor, as I heard him three years ago when a friend brought to the doctor's house an old field hand who had pneumonia, "Nigger, what's so wrong with you to disturb a doctor at night?" It is what you see in the school auditorium, one night in 1955, when the fathers of your schoolmates sit on a stage before a crowded audience and organize a Citizens Council to punish fifty Negroes who had signed an NAACP petition: no jobs, no loans, no groceries. It is the silence from the churches when two delta ruffians kill a Negro child from Chicago for looking at a white woman. It is the student at the state university saying of Faulkner, who had noted that a society which condones the killing of little children not only does not deserve to survive but probably will not, that he is a crazy drunk hot in pursuit of Northern money, and that his books make no sense anyway.

The average white Mississippian has no more natural evil or savagery than the average West German or Englishman or citizen of Yonkers, New York. Having been nurtured on his hate and shared in it, I have little cause for self-righteousness. What I do have is a monstrous shame, and I know full well that, trapped in its own institutionalized hate, landlocked in it like some dead and ancient sea, Mississippi is doomed to yet greater shame and violence.

II

The one hope concerning Mississippi lies in its progressive isolation from the rest of the South. This is happening now. There are deep forces at work in other Southern states which are largely absent in Mississippi. (Alabama may still be adamant, but at least it has an industrial Birmingham.) So far as I can see, the growing enlightenment of its younger white generation, which one occasionally hears about, is a fiction; enlightenment has been at a certain premium, at any rate, on the University of

Mississippi campus. The educated young whites are leaving the state almost as rapidly as the more restless young Negroes. The whites of the "educated" class who stay behind, in the experience of my hometown, are those young men whose fathers have set them up in the tire or used car or cotton business, and whose sense of independence is not what one would call Gandhian. On visits back home they drive you into corners. They have fire in their eyes. They want to make sure you haven't *changed*. "If I let my kids go to school with niggers," one of the up-and-coming young deacons at the Methodist Church told my wife, "how will they know they're better than the niggers?" Some argue, as a young man from Florida told me at a gathering in San Francisco recently, that all the trouble comes from the rednecks, the Snopses. But I have seen enough solid middle-class hatred in Mississippi to last a lifetime.

It was difficult to be surprised by the violence which broke out last fall at the University of Mississippi. Ole Miss is an institutional symbol, a pseudo-genteel outpost of brainless young beauties, incipient drunks, and winning football teams. Faulkner was not allowed to speak there. The rioting and the mayhem, of course, would have destroyed the school's reputation, if it had had one; it could lose its accreditation and not know it. The occasional good student who graduates from Ole Miss usually leaves the state, never to come back. A friend of mine, a Rhodes Scholar from Ole Miss, had been assured by three faculty members before he left for England to do an advanced law degree that the two or three courses he still lacked for his undergraduate law degree at Mississippi would automatically be absolved when he passed his examinations in England. He was a bright young man, full of the regional courtesies, but with an uncommon amount of independence. He thought he might come home and go into Mississippi politics. In the course of two years, as it happened, the three professors who had advised him at Ole Miss had either left the place or been driven out. He had to come back to finish his undergraduate work, and when I visited him at Ole Miss the summer he had come home from England, he was spending all his time outside of class getting drunk in front of an electric fan. (It is an axiom of survival that when the exile returns to Mississippi, he gets by on bootleg bourbon, usually chased with legal beer.) He had tried, he said, to keep to himself and get out as quickly as possible, but he was becoming more and more subject to wild outbursts in the school cafeteria against the smug young racists who had been praising Eastland and Barnett's good form on television from the Democratic national convention. Now my friend lives in New York.

As for what is happening among the school's faculty, one can only wonder. Some newspaper would be performing a public service if it conducted a survey among the professors at the University of Mississippi to find out how many are staying and how many leaving. Academicians in America are not particularly noted for an excess of verve, but after the events of the last few months, the ones at Mississippi must at least fear for the inviolability of their wives and children, if not for their own honor. A professor at a California university tells me that he looked around for one, but failed to find a single member of the Ole Miss English faculty at the convention of English professors in Washington last December. This convention, I understand, is a kind of national employment pool; it is where young teachers are recruited. But it would take a man of superhuman qualities, no doubt, to persuade a teacher to pay his scholarship on a battlefield.* Isolation from the American intellectual community, isolation from civilized values, isolation from the rest of the South seem almost inevitable for Mississippi.

III

Many Texans were disturbed to acknowledge that their state's major contribution to the Ole Miss riots was not the unalloyed criticism of most of its daily press, or the telegram from the student leaders at the University of Texas praising Meredith for his courage, or the student demonstrations supporting Meredith, or the many public statements from teachers and clergymen assailing the actions of the Mississippians, but General Edwin Walker's call to violence. Walker, who got more than 135,000 votes for governor of Texas the previous summer, summoned all good

---

*A well-known New York journalist who recently spent several days on the campus told me the administration is having an extremely difficult time finding replacements for the many professors who are leaving. Vacancies are being filled with academic driftwood. Of the eight white students who shared meals with Meredith in the school cafeteria during the fall semester, not a single one is now enrolled.

citizens to join him in the Battle of Ole Miss. He succeeded in drawing forth a more active segment of the underside of Southern humanity, for whom he ranks as the leading statesman. One of the out-of-state militiamen who must have been stirred by his call to rebellion came to Mississippi from Georgia, the wire services reported, and sat near a dormitory window during the rioting, firing into the crowds. Groups of little boys roamed the streets of the town, where Faulkner's *Intruder in the Dust* had been filmed a few years before, throwing rocks and bottles. Walker climbed a Confederate statue on the campus and said, "I want to compliment you on the protest you have made here tonight. You have a right to protest under the Constitution." Later, when the violence and bloodshed were at high tide, he asked the mob not to continue: "This," he said, "is not the road to Cuba." They jeered him down. In the end the "swelling response" which Walker found his appeal to have inspired consisted of chronic racists armed with .22's, rednecks armed with pipes and bludgeons, fraternity boys armed with stones, all crazy with hate and smelling blood. The "honor of the Confederacy" was on exhibit.

Texas had little cause to rejoice in this deranged contribution. Yet in its basic aspects, Texas is another world from Mississippi. It is as pluralistic as Mississippi is monolithic; it is free, it stimulates dissent, things are happening. For the past two years I was editor of a leftward weekly there, *The Texas Observer*. Since I came to California several people have inquired, in a civil, campus way, if it did not take an undue amount of courage to publish an outspoken journal in the South. In Mississippi I admit it would take more courage than I now have at my disposal, but in Texas it takes no courage at all. At the time we were operating on a healthy subsidy,* and our freedom to express ourselves was absolute. We were read by most of the state's intellectuals and by the great majority of the practicing politicians. As the only influential liberal publication in the state (there were two or three other weeklies of that persuasion) *The Observer* found itself something of a revered institution in its own country. State government itself is an anachronism, a great deal of sound and fury exerted in a vacuum, but not so the provincial politics of reform,

---

*But no longer. The paper has gone fortnightly, and under the excellent editorship of Ronnie Dugger is paying its own way, which is unusual to the point of sacrilege.

which is increasingly embracing the important national and international issues. And although Texas is still the citadel of some of the most corrosive wealth known to man, it has produced an impressive number of hard-headed political activists, young liberal and radical intellectuals. Texas has become, in the post-War years, an industrial, urban society; its labor-liberal-Negro-Mexican coalition, tenacious and growing, is setting an example for other of the more progressive states of the South. The strength of this coalition, within a developing two-party system, was clearly demonstrated in the Democratic primaries last summer when a young Houston lawyer, Don Yarborough, conducting the most completely liberal campaign of any statewide candidate in the South in this century, got 49 percent of the 1.2 million votes. On statewide television, Yarborough said he favored an end to radical discrimination—"both public and private." In Mississippi, a mere 300 miles to the east, this declaration would not have gone unchallenged (in fact, I am not sure the man would have survived it); in Texas it did. Racism is dead in statewide campaigning. The Negro bloc, increasingly numerous and well-organized, finds itself courted by all factions.

Although there is a distressingly long way to go, the lesson to be learned from Texas is that the one indispensable instrument for meaningful advancement of the Negro is the franchise. The hope for racial justice in the Southern states most assuredly does not lie in some imaginary curing of the Southern split-personality (whatever that may be; although writers like Robert Penn Warren seem to argue from that thesis). Nor does it lie, as other white Southern liberals vaguely suggest, in the forging in fire, with each passing racial crisis, of the white man's psyche. I am more concerned with what happens to Meredith's psyche, and others like him. It lies primarily, as a first step, in the Negro vote. Without the vote, all those goals which the Negro, with his white ally, has set for himself remain politically inaccessible; with it, the Negro can become less and less the ward of the white man.

In the meantime, one can only feel a deep admiration for the new generation of young Negroes in the South. The Negro undergraduates picketing the theaters at the University of Texas (and winning), the 187 students whose conviction for demonstrating in front of the South Carolina capitol has just been reversed by the Supreme Court, the young children who face the mobs every September, Meredith surrounded and insulted in the Ole Miss cafeteria—these courageous young souls embody today, in their honor and dignity, the best and most enduring of the Southern tradition itself. The South would do well to be proud of them; perhaps someday, in the far future, it will.

Bridgehampton

THE SOUNDS AND THE SILENCES

BRIDGEHAMPTON, N.Y.—Most of us who live more or less in solitude deserve a place of our own, outside the house, to visit when the gloom of home deepens with the early dark, where we can remain as private as we desire, lifting the veils of silence whenever we want to. That place for me is a saloon named Bobby Van's, an angular structure on Main Street with dark paneling, Tiffany lamps and old fans suspended from an undistinguished ceiling, a long mahogany bar, and from the back the flickering of candles on small booths and tables covered with red tablecloths. This is a village of dogs, big country dogs with melancholy faces who roam about unencumbered—all honored local personalities—and it is indicative of the notability of Bobby Van's that they always come in packs and scratch on the front door, wanting to be let inside.

I first met Bobby one night three years ago. He was standing guard over a corpse, a man run over on the road outside, and while we waited in this death-watch for the coroner, I learned that Bobby was a dropout from The Juilliard School, a pianist since the age of five, who decided somewhere along the way that he wanted his own baby-grand in his own bar.

He is a native Long Islander, a short, dark young man in his early thirties, with a look in his eyes of the hunter squinting out from the brush—loyal to all, full of good graces: well brought up, as we would have said in the South. He knows almost everyone worth knowing among the perpetual residents from Hampton Bays to Montauk, and for that matter a few not worth knowing at all. He wears a white chef's suit when he is cooking in the kitchen, and he comes most to life when he is playing his piano, at home with Vivaldi or Cole Porter—sometimes in the summer to a packed house of New Yorkers who have frightened the locals away, but usually this time of year to ten or twelve of us who have come in out of the cold.

Unlike other places I know intimately, the Lord's abiding language does not run deep here, and we know each other so well by now that our talk is more by gesture than by word. Those of us who come here value Bobby for providing us with this unprepossessing refuge, which is usually as civilized as the best English pub, although some patrons have been known to be unshaven.

Bobby knows the tempos and cadences of this native place—a place that, being a resort in summer, changes character more drastically with the seasons than any stretch of earth I have ever known. Only once have I seen him embarrassed by the treacheries of nature here, when the Coast Guard hauled him in after he was lost in Gardiner's Bay for eight hours (several of us waited anxiously in the saloon for word of him, meanwhile helping ourselves to free drinks), and even then he brought back enough bluefish for everybody. He knows the flights of the geese and the next big change in the wind. People come here to find out where the fish are running, they wander in with ducks they have shot to be dressed and eaten, and like our predecessors who sought out deep caves and built fires in them, we come to Bobby's to huddle together during storms.

One bitter night many months ago, a dog who was my brother and is long since dead—a black Labrador named I. H. Crane now buried by the pond he loved the best—darted out of Bobby's saloon where we had all been sitting; he stayed gone for a long time. I said I was worried. "I just heard him," Bobby said, with the certitude of the country mystic. We ran to Bobby's old white Cadillac with the missing muffler, sped at least a mile down country lanes, stopping suddenly at a remote spot then unknown to me. Bobby Van opened the door, and in an instant I. H. Crane emerged from the icy thickets and jumped in beside us, nuzzling us with a frozen nose.

Bobby knows who is sick and who has died, the consummated loves and the broken ones. He is the public servitor of a village without a newspaper. Like many of my friends here, he is shaped by the winter land, shedding that skin like a Mississippi swamp snake when the summer begins and the influx comes. He does not have to go to the ocean every day to remember it is there.

I discovered this area by accident, from the back of a chartered bus a few years ago, with advertising salesmen from *Harper's* going to Montauk for a conference. In a lethargy that day, I glanced out my window; things flickering obliquely before my eyes brought me awake: lush potato fields on the flat land, village greens, old graveyards, shingled houses, ancient elms along the streets, and far in the distance the blue Atlantic breakers. It was the unfolding of one's profoundest dreams, and I knew then I would come back here someday for a long time.

It is likely the most beautiful terrain in America, and because of that, and its proximity to Manhattan eighty miles down the road, I am afraid it will become a parking lot. In summertime the New Jersey plates grow more and more abundant, and this is always a fearsome sign. From an airplane at a thousand feet flying into the city, one sees the higher civilization coming out this way: earth ripped raw, shopping centers, developments, all the immense apparatus at the edge of the great American schizophrenia. There is a mean Australian boy with a Ph.D. on the environment fighting for its survival, and if anyone can do it he can, but I fear for its doom.

I place no blame indiscriminately, and certainly not self-righteously, for this is a complicated matter. But once at Bobby Van's I asked a young potato farmer why he had sold the acreage up the way to W. T. Grant's, which would soon install its largest store in the East. "Because my grandmama and I are out for one thing," he said, "and that's the buck." I could not quarrel with that. Instead, after a tender silence, on a napkin I wrote from Faulkner's "The Bear": "The ruined woods we used to know don't cry for retribution. Then men who have destroyed it will accomplish its revenge." The young landowner pondered this message; I could tell he was turning it about in his mind. Then he said: "I *knew* you were with me."

It is a land that enlists loneliness, and also love. It reminds me a little of the Mississippi Delta, without the Delta blood and guilt—no violence to this land, and it demands little. The village itself remains part of the land that encompasses it. When my young son comes from the city he walks all over town talking with the farmers and the merchants; the lovely young daughter of a friend gave me for Christmas an autograph book, with inscriptions to me from all the people who work on Main

Street, and from all the children here her age. One day before it snowed I noticed from my car this simple tableau: my son on the sloping lawn next to Bobby Van's, having sandwiches for lunch with Spindley, Bobby's ubiquitous golden retriever. The boy and the dog sat there on the grass, motionless almost, in the golden sunshine of a crisp December noon, and the sight of them as I spied upon them in their unaffected pose evoked in a mellow rush my own small-town childhood.

It is a very small town here in the winter, numbering just over a thousand people. Just as the potato fields bring back the Mississippi Delta, the village reminds me of my home Yazoo, because along the streets in daylight and in darkness, there are the sounds of Negro voices, all the vanished echoes of one's youth. It is nearly 30 percent black, mostly Southerners; its public school is almost entirely colored, and one of the sadnesses of the town is that it does not have the despair and cruelty and tragedy of remembrance; it lacks the shared past, the common inheritance of the land, that has helped Yazoo survive. A generation ago the farmers brought them out here, and then spurned them.

There is an old Negro man here whom we all know, who perambulates around town at all hours, drinking Thunderbird behind hedges and trees, talking incessantly to himself, head aslant in his aimless journey. No one knows where he sleeps, if he does at all. Eight or ten times a day I see him, one moment down by the tracks, five minutes later in the graveyard, then near the church, then in front of Bobby Van's, and I have even sighted him as far away as Sag Pond and the ocean. Being a Southern boy, I must believe he is a reminder to the town of something it does not truly know of itself, but many here would not wholly understand what I mean. My son and the lovely girl who gave me the autograph book spotted him, alone as always, on Christmas Day, and ran out to give him a present in a bottle.

The holidays were over; the people from Washington and New York were going back, one's friends from a more public past. I could see them as their cars sped westward on the Montauk Highway. All around, the countryside was deep in snow, the bare branches heavy with ice, and on this bleak wisp of a day the flat fields stretching toward the ponds and the ocean filled one with a wrenching desolation. Soon there would be children skating in the low wet places in the fields, and the sight of a solitary farmer surveying his terrain. Now there was no movement. I drove with a girl I loved over the same lanes of our summer; the girl wanted one last look at the winter beach, the sea tossed by a north wind, the dunes more grey than white under the ponderous skies. Then she, too, was gone. Later I watched my young son climb on the 3 o'clock train for the city—and I remained for a moment on the platform as the train rumbled through the snowbanks and disappeared around the bend.

I trudged up Main Street toward my car, feeling again that acid dryness in the throat, almost sexual to the senses, of being left somehow behind. *Who am I? What am I doing here?* Bobby Van's saloon was dark and empty in that hour, yet from far inside it I heard music. I cupped my hands against the big window and saw Bobby in the gloom, sitting at the baby grand. I walked on. Fifty yards away the sounds of Chopin still drifted across the snow.

Prelude to Setting Off in a Camper to History

Every time I live in Washington for a while, I find myself looking for the common things that hold Americans together. It's not even a conscious thing, and my mind never particularly worked that way when I served my stretch on Manhattan Island. But last night at sunset, going to look at the Jefferson Memorial on Washington's Birthday with my sixteen-year-old son David visiting from New York City and a friend who lives among the potato fields of Long Island and his fifteen-year-old boy whom we call Jamie, it was no surprise that the talk turned to that thin skein which holds the civilization together.

I suppose that's not a bad topic for fathers and sons to talk about around here at this time of the year.

My friend is a student of all this who just moved his family back to America after fifteen years on the Isle St. Louis in Paris. He smokes nauseating cigars and once wrote a book called *From Here to Eternity* and another called *The Thin Red Line,* and wherever he goes he carries several knives he got off the Japs at Guadalcanal. The four of us are about to take a red pick-up truck with a camper in the back down to Chancellorsville, Spotsylvania, and the Wilderness to listen to the rustlings of the ghosts of eighteen-year-old boys, and then on to Harper's Ferry and Antietam, from which the next report, God willing, will emanate, unless the writer vanishes into those terrible old echoes of the Sunken Road.

My friend and I discovered as we looked across the Potomac from our pick-up truck that Washington reminds us both of Rome—not that it's as old as ancient Rome or that it even looks much like Rome, but that it too may someday many years from now be ruins, and that some future scholar may conclude there probably was some kind of public meeting place here.

Not that we for a moment wished it, Lord knows, especially in that spectacular twilight and in the company of our two American boys, and I'm sure we would get down on our knees and pray, if that could do it, that our hegemony will endure.

Surely it is the most beautiful edifice in Washington. The memorial to Kennedy has more activity inside, and the one to Lincoln is more solid, but this one more perfectly catches the spirit of the man and his age. One day last year, touring the rooms of Monticello with other visitors, under the guidance of one of those charming Virginia ladies who always call him "Mister Jefferson," David and I overheard a woman from the Bronx say to her husband, after we had borne witness to Mr. Jefferson's sixteenth invention: "He must have been some weird weirdo." Well, he was not, and as I watched Jamie and David go on ahead up the steps and start reading the words on the walls of his Memorial, I felt happy that he was around when he was, and even made a secret wish that he were here today, either here in this town right now or trampling about in the snows of New Hampshire if necessary.

Of the five quotations on the wall, Jamie said he liked the one that comes out against the commerce in human slavery best. I asked him why, and this fine boy who was born and raised in Paris and is also like a son to me, and who plays leftfield for a softball team we have on Long Island called the Golden Nematodes consisting of bartenders, potato farmers, writers, and boys (David plays centerfield), said because it makes such good sense.

I think David's favorite is the one which talks about the truths they held to be self-evident, although he says he hasn't made up his mind. Personally, I find myself partial to the promise he swore on the altar of God. My friend, who threw away his cigar before he went inside, likes every one of them, or I got that impression from the look on his face when he was reading them all, and by the fact that he dwelt on them for a very long time.

Later, the four of us went out on the steps and admired that majestic view you get from there against the burnt orange sky. Jamie said that once when he was a little boy he wandered around the forum at Rome at night time and got scared, and on top of that some scrawny stray cats who inhabit those pits came after him. That got David on the subject of a dismal afternoon we spent years ago at Stonehenge. My friend said he didn't have enough time to think of all that on Guadalcanal, but he did later when they shipped him back to the military hospital in Memphis, Tennessee.

It was a good prelude to that country we are heading for, where all of this nearly washed away in blood. It was just a father-and-son sort of thing on Washington's Birthday.

The South and Welcome to It

Does It Still Exist?

Not too long ago I got a letter from a friend, a fellow of early middle age from the Deep South who had dwelled in the North for many years and had recently returned to live in a big overgrown city of Dixie. Since I had also left and returned, my friend posed a few questions to me that had obviously been bothering him, as if he had made the wrong decision about his own repatriation or, worse, had responded to his spiritual reckoning without regard, as the lawyers say, to the true facts of things.

"I wonder if the South as we once knew it still exists—if there *is* a South anymore," he said. "This is a question I've been getting from friends of mine. I think that's new. I don't know what the reason is— maybe those media creations called the Sunbelt and the New South—but I sense that people here are feeling more a part of the wider world than ever before. They profess to feel less a part of that old concept you and I know as 'The South.'"

I could not deny his observations. Once the albatross of race, in its more suffocating aspects, was removed, Southerners became free as never before to feel part of the broader civilization, and that is good. The American South, after all, is merely one region among many on the Lord's Earth as it swirls out at the edge of the universe, sharing immutably in the fears and terrors that haunt the human race. But that change is hard for some of us to appreciate.

"I, too, have been asking myself questions," my friend continued. "Is the idea of 'The South' felt by anyone besides writers and other people who spend too much time thinking about themselves? Is it nothing more than personal nostalgia codified? Are Virginians and Mississippians connected by anything other than the fact that their ancestors lost a war together? What *is* innately Southern anymore?"

And his concluding observation, which caused me at least one long and sleepless night: "Do you wish you could escape it again?"

There is much of the South, I unhesitatingly confess to him, that I wish I could escape forever. I wish I could escape the smoldering malevolence behind a coed's prolonged racial tirade among students at my house one recent evening. Escape the tenacious righteousness of the "seg academies." Escape the images of the catastrophic destruction, physical and communal, of places like my beloved Austin in Texas. Escape every manifestation of institutionalized, right-wing, fundamentalist religion, richer and more pervasive than it ever was. Escape the ennui of the morgue-like Sundays. Escape the fruitless spleen and irrelevant innuendo of the intellectual discourse.

To escape the South, however—all of what it was and is—I would have to escape from myself.

One of the central themes in our history as Americans, reflected in our most enduring literature, has been the conflict between country and city, the dichotomy between village and metropolis, with all that that embraces. With the homogeneity engendered by the great television culture, and the growing power of the mighty urban nexus, that gulf remains a profound one. Nowhere is this more emphatic than in the contemporary South, in which raw old towns have become cities in less than our lifetime, and the countryside and the villages are portrayed as languishing near death. Modern forces seem to have conspired against the small-town South of our memory, just as they have nowadays against the rural Midwest.

There is a price to be paid for that, and it may be entirely more than was bargained for. Big cities are big cities anywhere, and it is the large and burgeoning cities of the South that becloud the more pristine consideration of roots, remembrance, and belonging. *Does the South any longer exist?* I have heard the plaintive cry time without number from the denizens of such cities as Atlanta, Memphis, Birmingham, and Houston, but I think not once in more than five years have I heard it from anyone living in Southern towns, or in their encompassing countryside.

Ironically, the horrendous exodus of Southerners of both races to the cities of the North has been reversed at a time when the rural South is in its bleakest stagnation—so much so that an artist of my acquaintance is doing paintings of dying Mississippi villages so future generations will know how they looked. Jobs are increasing twice as fast in the urban areas of the South as in the small towns. In Georgia, three-fourths of all new employment since 1980 has been in the Atlanta region alone. The same is true in Arkansas, where, in the midst of a rural depression, Little Rock's per capita income is above the national average and unemployment is below it. But in the rural South, joblessness is now 37 percent above the American norm.

The decline in the Southern rural economy is especially difficult, as such things always are, on the blacks. Those places in the South experiencing the most rapid growth are those whose workers are the best educated. The rural South has always been the least educated region in America. Illiteracy remains common, and only one-fourth of the population twenty-five or older has high school diplomas. Yet in Mississippi, for example, after sharp decreases in the state budget under a governor who adamantly opposes tax increases of any kind, the eight state universities are eliminating doctoral programs and ordering layoffs as well as reductions and freezes in salaries. Alcorn State University, a black institution, has suffered a 28 percent decrease in its budget. "Hope is not all we need," Faulkner wrote. "It's all we got." I daresay no other region in the United States can still say that with impunity.

I am reminded of a recent conversation I had with an acquaintance of mine, a native of the Midwest, who runs the Atlanta bureau of one of the nation's largest newspapers. He had been doing a story out in the Mississippi Delta, where time has stood still, and he had been touched by the patina of this older, inward South. The Delta had bewildered and intrigued him, for it has always both frightened and titillated the outsider.

"It's the other extreme from Atlanta," he said. "Southerners hate to be strangers to each other. That's why Atlanta is so traumatic for Southerners to visit. Southerners like to see you and say, 'Hi, how are you?' And the Yankees in Atlanta just don't respond to that. As for the native Atlantans, there's a city they remember that no longer really exists. But they still see it as if it were there—the gracious cotillions, the old Rich's department store, the old Peachtree Street, the Buckhead Boys." He remembered what one old Atlantan had said to him: "Maybe my city is only the way I remember it in my mind."

Yet is it not similarly true that the great Southern cities of the 1980s are like the artistic effect called pentimento? To quote Lillian Hellman, who wrote a wonderful book by that name, "Old paint on canvas, as it ages, sometimes becomes transparent. When that happens it is possible, in some pictures, to see original lines: a tree will show through a woman's dress, a child makes way for a dog, a large boat is no longer on an open sea." So beneath the palpable new "sophistication" of these contemporary Southern cities, can one not find the Conroes, Lake Villages, Belzonis, Mebanes, Humboldts, Valdostas, Eufalas, Guthries, Bastrops, and Farmvilles? Nostalgia is not what it used to be, it has been remarked, yet nostalgia is mere saccharin to the Southerner's power of memory—for memory is everything.

Walker Percy once wrote that at a certain point in his life a man draws strength from living in some authentic relationship with the principal events of his past. I have often pondered what it was that brought me back to stay. I am forever drawn to the textures, the echoes, the way things look and feel, the bittersweet tug of certain phrases: "We crossed the river at Natchez." The South is a blend of the relentless and the abiding for me, and an accumulation of ironies so acute and impenetrable that my vagabond heart palpitates to make sense of them.

There is indisputably something in the shared topography. But to find it, one must get off the interstates at every chance, as I always do, and as I did on an early day of homecoming into the Delta. It was a bitterly cold forenoon of January, so cold that huge shards of ice were in the rivers and creeks, and under the somber skies in the seared fields the vacated tenant shacks were ghostly and bereft. There was a black funeral in a graveyard near the road. Amid the homemade tombstones with the misspelled inscriptions, the pallbearers were struggling to carry the cheap pine coffin up an incline, and three little children stood crying under a water oak. Farther on, in a sudden wintry wind, was the little all-black village of Falcon with its brand new water tower, black kids with socks on their hands shooting baskets, and lean-to vistas.

Then the main street of Alligator with its boarded-up storefronts—had everyone migrated to Greenville or Indianola? Out from town the cotton stubble was gray and frozen, and I knew with the springtime these fields would be worked by the enormous new tractors with air conditioners and stereos in their cabins. I made a side tour to Drew to visit a friend, but she had been out in the swamps most of the night killing bullfrogs with a .22 pistol for a frog-fry and had remained at her girlfriend's house in the country. Now past the big white houses surrounded by pecans and magnolias with croquet lawns, tennis courts, and swimming pools, and a couple of Mercedes and pick-up trucks under the porticoes. South out of the Delta to Raymond, my familial village, founded by my people, suffused with evanescent rustlings for me—the crumbling cemetery, the railroad bridge on which my grandfather proposed to my grandmother in 1897, my great-grandparents' house, which ran red with blood when my great-grandmother nursed the wounded of both sides and took down a letter from a dying Illinois boy to his mother and saw that it got through the lines. Then back into America again on Interstate 20 West. At twilight in the bar overlooking the river in Vicksburg a man from Iowa asked me, "Say, wasn't there some kind of battle here?"

I am afraid that I can answer by original correspondent only elliptically, if indeed at all. At the risk of all generalizations of the spirit, and of incurring the displeasure of some among my fellow Americans, indulge me in this brief catalog—a few of the qualities that, in my own, most personal view, still make the South different, or at the least are more characteristic of the South than of other regions. I have been looking around these past years, have kept an eye cocked for the abiding nuance, and if I am wrong, I am not *too* wrong.

• A heightened sense of community, of mutuality. To this day, when Southerners get together, no matter where, be it Richmond, Washington, New York, or London, they do not wish merely to exchange pleasantries or casual information. Listen to them. They are seeking background on families, relatives, friends, events, landmarks, memories. They know somebody who knows somebody. Things are going on at different levels in this sly, subtle premonition of kindredship.

• Manners. They are more carefully, almost cunningly, plotted and handed down, a gentle and genteel response to the complexities of life, an improvisation, a way of keeping the sudden and unexpected and threatening at bay, of coping with pain and the uncharted.

• Ritual. Southerners remain more ritualistic than most other Americans. It is a ritualism that springs from old rhythms and cadences and from the earth, or from one's memory of the earth—funerals, marriages, baptisms, betrothals, friendships, loyalties, rivalries. They like football in this country, but in the South even football is a folk ritual touching on religiosity, and Saturday is a holy day.

• A stronger feeling of morality. Not the morality of the Falwells and the Helmses, but an inherited incentive that says you are your brother's keeper, that you must try and take care of one another, that you must share a comforting mutual security. And with this comes a crafty and artful sense of sin that in my lifetime has not noticeably softened. Fundamentalism still makes sinning more forbidden, and hence more pleasurable. The liquor signs at the precise county lines of wet precincts are as ubiquitous as ever, as if Satan himself is beckoning the wanderer.

• Whites and blacks trying to live together within a common history. Although many of the changes in the lives of black Southerners have been cosmetic ones, and they remain on the day-to-day level the most impoverished Americans, something meaningful is happening here. Who could have predicted a generation ago, when the Civil Rights Movement was at its crest, that the integration of the public schools would someday work best in the small-to middle-size cities in the South? It is the world of proms and cheerleading and classrooms and ball games. A black Ole Miss football player, dying of leukemia, asks to be buried in his letter-sweater. A white and black homecoming court stands at attention to the strains of a high school alma mater. A white high school boy named Jaybird in the town where I live has his mother make him cornbread every day so his jumpshots will be as effective as those of his black teammates. The teammates—Topcat, Toady, and Weasel—come to his house to do homework and to eat the cornbread, too.

• Finally, continuity. I passionately believe that there is an ineluctable continuity to Southern experience that still exists; I see it everywhere. It is a matter of the stories passed along, of the music and the speech, of knowing who lives in such-and-such house and who lived there before, and where the wisteria grows best and the robin eats her first crocus. "If you have one distinguished ancestor," Barry Hannah says, "Southerners will never forget it, and you won't either." A white father I know wants his son to go north to college, but in his secret heart hopes he will come home someday. A black mayor of a small Mississippi town remembers standing by the roadside as a child, her grandmother waving down a Greyhound to take them north: "And that highway still looks pretty much the same. It was such a thrill because that bus just came out of nowhere, and when you got on it you knew you were going someplace. But now when I go someplace far away, and I'm headed back, I see that road and it looks like home."

Does the south exist any longer? One has to seek the answer on one's own terms, of course, but to do that, I suggest, one should spurn the boardrooms and the country clubs and the countless college seminars on the subject and spend a little time at the ball games and the funerals and the bus stations and the courthouses and the bargain-rate beauty parlors and the little churches and the roadhouses and the joints near the closing hour.

I did not judge the South remotely dead in a roadhouse near Vicksburg on a recent Saturday of the full moon. The parking lot was filled with pick-up trucks. That afternoon, only a mile beyond the hill, they had put 20,000 miniature American flags on the Union dead in the battlefield for Memorial Day, and the bar talk was vivid on this and other things. Dozens of couples in all modes of dress gyrated on the dance floor to Willie Nelson tunes, and the unprepossessing interior echoed with wild greetings and indigenous hosannas. There was a pride in this place that I knew in my ancestral soul, a pride not to be unduly tampered with, and if you had had the mettle to ask one of those people if the South still existed on that night, he would have stared you up and down and replied: "Who *you*, boy?"

I know a black South African student whom the Soviets courted at the University of Moscow before he decided to take a fellowship here. I enjoy watching the South through his eyes. "When I first came, I was afraid I'd made a big mistake," he says. "But the South grows on you. It seems so removed, but it's vividly real. I'll miss it when I go home. I don't understand why your national media wants a uniform U.S.A."

Nor, for that matter, do I. But I can testify to the hostility and ambivalence toward the South that still exists in many areas of the nation. Is it the lingering fear of differentness? I testify also to my own self-ironies, for when I dwelled in the North I felt more Southern than I ever had before; back home again to stay, I feel more American.

Perhaps in the end it is the old, inherent, devil-may-care instinct of the South that remains in the most abundance and will sustain the South in its uncertain future. The reckless gambler's instinct that fought and lost that war, Snake Stabler calling a bootleg play on fourth down, a Texas wildcatter putting his stakes on the one big strike, a black mother working sixteen hours a day to educate her children, a genteel matron borrowing from the banker to send her daughter to a university sorority so she can marry well. It is gambling with the heart, it is a glass menagerie, it is something that won't let go.

In a Shifting Interlude

*How ungenerously in later life we disclaim the virtuous moods of our youth,
living in retrospect long summer days of unreflecting dissipation, Dresden figures of pastoral gaiety! Our wisdom, we prefer to think, is all of our own
gathering, while, if the truth be told, it is, most of it, the last coin of a legacy
that dwindles with time.*

—Evelyn Waugh, *Brideshead Revisited*

I have not been back in more than thirty years. The old, brave, magnificent town is suffused for me with youth and death, and forever imbued
in my memory with an uncommon maze of emotions, some felicitous,
others premonitory. Quite frankly, I am a little afraid of the incontrovert-
ible burden of its past, and of memory itself, to go back again. There are
old, buried fears of it. Is my return certain to be strange and magic and
sad?

My new wife, JoAnne, a Mississippi girl of kindly and percipient dis-
position, is with me on this bizarre odyssey. She has visited Oxford once,
she tells me, in 1968 for three and a half hours. I remind her that I have
once visited there also, for three and a half years, this in the late 1950s,
peremptorily dispatched there with my American contemporaries by
Cecil Rhodes as one of "the best men for the world's fight." There is an
extant photograph of the thirty-two of us Rhodes scholars, on a golden
autumn's forenoon on the deck of *The Flandre* in our crossing, the purple,
sun-crossed Atlantic breakers as background. The boys of that long-ago
passage are all over fifty now, and occasionally I ponder that picture
and conjure Lord Lindsay's collective eulogy to his fellow Cambridge
Olympians of '24 in *Chariots of Fire*, for we too must have had "hopes in
our hearts and wings on our heels." These were the Eisenhower years,
and America was doing fine. The dollar lasted a long time. The hegem-

ony of the big green passport swept all before it. In this peacetime cadre there are to be no war tragedies, no incipient mayhems, merely the natural demises and the simple attritions of mortal time.

We encountered there an England still in the ruin of war. And in Oxford we confronted one of the preeminent universities of the world, if not *the* foremost, in its inwardness and nuance and sweep, a nexus far removed from our native ground, where the measure was more languid and the aspect more subtle and elusive, a repository of the dire complexities of mankind. The sacrosanct privacy of the place, the almost studied eccentricities, the enervating fogs and rains, at first elicited a loneliness, an angst and melancholia such as I had never known before. The advanced civility of our new milieu, the weight of its history, where every blade of grass had known a dozen drops of blood, the Old World tensions, seemed cloying and troublesome, and the mementos of mortality were everywhere, in the lugubrious graveyards, in the interminable rolls of the war dead in the college chapels, in the dampened dusks and spooky midnights.

The university itself had begun to evolve in the eleventh century, and by the fifteenth its zealously independent colleges, rich and fortresslike and autonomous with their own histories and constituencies and prerogatives, were in exotic flourish. In AD 1991 these colleges number thirty-five, serving nearly 14,000 students. Has any single place on earth of comparable size produced such an august array of human beings? The catalog is endless; to try to list them, and the stupendous accomplishments they shaped there, would be futile, but imagine the oppressiveness of their footfalls as their spirits stalked a callow young American a generation or so ago. "Oxford is a city of many kinds," Jan Morris has written in her classic *Oxford*, one of my favorite books, "and the look of the place varies: sometimes noble, sometimes ugly, sometimes edible, sometimes hole-in-corner, sometimes full of surprises and sometimes only suggestive of things that have happened here, or great men who have passed this way." These and other things "raise this University and its patron city into the upper ranks of human artifacts, up there with the works of art, the codes of laws and philosophies."

The essence of the Oxford system was, and remains, the tutorial, in which the student, after intensive reading, writes weekly or twice-weekly essays and defends them in private sessions with his college tutor, or don. Examinations are comprehensive and come at the end of three years, six hours a day for more than two weeks. Lectures are optional, one of the English students having explained to me that they had gone out of fashion with the invention of the printing press in the fifteenth century. Yet the voluminous lecture list for each of the three yearly terms would defy the most eclectic imagination. For Trinity Term, 1991, from a book-length roster I especially sighted: Experimental Archaeology and the Perform-ance of Ancient Boats; A Neo-Dumezilian Approach to Hinduism; Oscan and Umbrian Texts; Holomorphic Vector Bundles; Readings in Pre-Mod-ern Yiddish Literature; Language Universals and Linguistic Typology; Acid-Base, Metal Ion, and Redox Equilibria; Philosophy and Politics from Hegel to Husseni and Heidegger; Historical and Analytical Enquir-ies; and United States Government and Politics under President Bush.

With the tutorial essay the only formal requirement, one might do as he pleased: read novels, write poetry, go to London, sleep till noon, or devote sixteen hours a day reading for the next tutorial. There was an abiding homage to independence and self-sufficiency, and to the paths one's mind took. I would be reading in my rooms in my college, and, under the tranquil allure of the ancient quadrangle out my window or of the Latin psalms of the boys' choirs in the chapel, lapse into endless reveries about home, or the past. It was not an uncommon malaise. "If the people at Annapolis knew how much I daydreamed in this place," a U.S. Naval Academy man in my group once confessed to me, "I'd be up for a court-martial."

Yet, slowly, the spell of Oxford grew, until one was suffused with it, with its majesty and largesse and thrall. We became Oxford men, and the elegiac and lofty mosaic of it would be part of us forever, and also the ambivalent misgiving.

It is extraordinary how the weather, not unlike smell, brings back so much of past moments to those of our species. The moist gray chill of Oxford enveloped me and evoked in a supple rush the memories of those days, and the people who shared them with me. And, of course, there is the Oxford rain—a teased, beguiling little drizzle more often than not, punctuated by fleet downpours, and then a charitable April sun will escape the cloud-banks and bathe the spires and pinnacles and domes in a gloaming. That is Oxford for me, its shifting interludes, all shadow and act.

It is springtime. The trees are still half-bare. The muted gray of the stone silhouettes amid the flowering bushes and shrubs, the lush green leaves and gardens greener beyond measure than the most opulent Aprils of the American South, bring a timelessness to the familiar hush. It is as if I am in a declivity of old time itself as I wander the town, for I recognize no one, and no one me, an anonymous wisp resurrected in the instant to explore the medieval lanes and byways and cul-de-sacs I once knew in my heart. A mist soon descends, and all about are the footsteps in the fog, and the echoes of young voices and laughter from strangers not even born when I was last here.

It is midafternoon of my first day here, and raining hard now, and JoAnne is incorrigibly American in a yellow rain cap and homely walking shoes and a gay green trenchcoat. There are already lights in the Bodleian and the Radcliffe Camera with their endless stacks of books and the young people burrowed in study at the long mahogany tables. The very façades of Ship Street, which intersects Jesus College and Saint Michael's Church with its grim Saxon tower, bring back to me a Sunday twilight years ago when I walked this downcast passage and suffered the memory of a girl I had left behind in America, and I can almost feel that vanished ache. In the Regency elegance of Beaumont Street, where Richard the Lion-Hearted was born, with its row upon row of dentists' offices, I remember Johnny D'Arms of Princeton inviting me to his flat here and gravely soliciting my counsel, as he withdrew clothes from a battered wardrobe, on which Ivy League suit to wear to Evelyn Waugh's country estate the next day to ask his daughter's hand in marriage. Whatever the suit we chose, a Princeton seersucker as I recall, it served the purpose. All about us in the city are the tucked-away Dickensian shops, a little forlorn at first sight, yet oddly ancillary to the business at hand of a distinguished university: antiquarian booksellers and numismatists and Indian art dealers and minuscule tailoring establishments, and at the foot of the Broad the inviting exterior of Blackwell's, the greatest bookstore in the world, whose forbearing proprietors once allowed me three years to satisfy my considerable arrears when I went home at last to America.

It is High Street itself, one of the most impressive in Europe in its eighteenth-century eminence, which reminds one anew that contemporary Oxford, encompassing its blood-proud colleges in every aspect and direction, is an industrial city of more than 115,000 people. I always admired the cobbled lanes that led away from it, to surreptitious dead ends with honest pubs and restaurants. Wordsworth was a Cambridge man— "the other place," as they call it here—who caught the High in his florid sonnet:

> *I slight my own beloved Cam, to range*
> *Where silver Isis leads my stripling feet;*
> *Pace the long avenue, or glide adown*
> *The stream-like windings of that glorious street—*

The motion along the High on this day is furious, with its multifarious vehicles and grinding motors and the edgy berating of a hundred horns, and wave upon wave of bicycles in a vicinage reputed to have more of them per capita than any place on the globe. If one wishes a more bucolic setting, he must go to Wordsworth's Cambridge. Yet much of the enduring verve of Oxford lies in this querulous juxtaposition of Town and Gown, for this university, unlike many others everywhere, has not, and indeed could not, even if it wished, withdraw into a quirky preciosity.

The bells are beginning to ring now, resonating in the precocious gloom. South of the High, only a few minutes' walk from its torrid clamor, the view of Christ Church and Merton from Broad Walk with its protective elms, then Dead Man's Walk with the Old City Wall standing gaunt and forbidding before us, was always to me the most imposing in Oxford, revealing the city and the colleges in their true origin: medieval, fortressed, embattled. In the diaphanous fog and rain we have this alluvial terrain all to ourselves: In the distance the miniature, childlike Thames, called *Isis* in the neighborhood, in its diffident twistings and turnings, and at the skyline the looming shape of tower and cupola and pinnacle. Often was the day I walked alone along these water paths, a little histrionically perhaps with a Matthew Arnold in hand, or a Lewis Carroll, who first told his Alice stories to the children on a boat somewhere along this stretch of river. And it may have been on this bench under this elm in a morning of June on the somnolent meadows that I read aloud to myself:

In a Wonderland they lie,
Dreaming as the days go by
Dreaming as the summers die.

Ever drifting down the stream—
Lingering in the golden gleam—
Life, what is it but a dream?

Entering the gateways of the Oxford colleges, one abruptly passes into another world. Six of the colleges—Magdalen, University, Queens, All Souls, Brasenose, and Oriel—abut on the High, and suddenly there they are, unhurried and intimate and smug beside the noisome modern commerce. It is the colleges that have always endowed Oxford with its quintessential complexion, their insular and self-contained quadrangles and gardens and dining halls and chapels. The college gardens with their sweeping lawns and herbaceous borders are magnificent in the waning afternoon. There are trees in flourishing pink and white, and budding horse chestnuts, and cedars and copper beeches, and tulips and daffodils and jonquils and pansies and Japanese magnolias and snapdragons on the walls, and everything drips heavily with moisture, so palpable that you can almost touch it in the gathering air.

On my return to these colleges, I cannot help associating them in my own clandestine memory with my faraway Yank contemporaries who once dwelled in them, for their presence on this day is everywhere: their laughter, their mischief, and comradeship. I knew these colleges best from visiting my friends there, dining as a guest on the same scrimpy fare in their medieval halls, drinking in their pubs, sometimes spending the night after the gates were padlocked at eleven p.m. It was in Merton College on one such evening that my friends and several of the English described the college ghosts, including the one who appeared one midnight to be walking on his knees in a room of the Old Quad. The students' reports were received with skepticism until an architectural survey disclosed that the original floor of the room, built in 1254, was eighteen inches below the present floor.

By such token, Oriel College, with its Jacobean Gothic contours and seventeenth-century quadrangle, is the college not only of Sir Walter Raleigh and Cecil Rhodes, but of Mike Hammond of Lawrence College, a former university president and now dean of the music school at Rice University, and Jess Wood of the University of Mississippi, the first of our class to die, who on taking me on a tour of his new estate commented, "I could do with a little less historical tradition and a few more modern conveniences." Sixteenth-century Brasenose is the precinct not of Lord Tweedsmuir, but of the star-touched Pete Dawkins, captain of the corps and Heisman Trophy halfback from West Point, later a Vietnam hero. Mighty thirteenth-century Balliol produced not merely Algernon Swinburne, but Paul "Tyke" Sarbanes of Princeton, later to be a U.S. senator. Sixteenth-century Jesus College was domicile not of Lawrence of Arabia but of Ed Yoder of Chapel Hill ("What a friend we have in Jesus," we said of him), Pulitzer Prize–winner. Fifteenth-century Magdalen with its splendid groves and meadows and river paths evoked for me not Oscar Wilde but the late Bob Childres of Ole Miss, legal scholar. Seventeenth-century Wadham, Jacobean Gothic with its deft classical touches, I identified not with Christopher Wren but with the Princetonian Charlie Fried, one day to be solicitor general of the United States. Christ Church, founded by Cardinal Wolsey in 1525 and the most grandiose of the Oxford colleges with its own cathedral and the Great Quadrangle inside its massive gateway, elicited for me not thirteen prime ministers nor, for that matter, William Penn, but Dick Baker, all-American swimmer of Chapel Hill, former prep-school headmaster. Thirteenth-century Merton, with the oldest chapel of them all and the dark, ghostly Mob Quad, 1308, which chilled me to the bone whenever I visited it, contributed not just T. S. Eliot and Max Beerbohm but Ed Selig of Yale, writer and lawyer, and Truman Schwartz, the University of South Dakota, chemist. During our first term here, Schwartz confided to me in a letter, "I look out my bedroom every morning, across Merton's front quad, just to make sure the chapel, which was built around 1290, is still standing. I think I expect to find it transmuted overnight into the Farmers' Cooperative grain elevator in Freeman, South Dakota." He would later tell me the chapel had become more real to him than the grain elevator, an admission I comprehend.

By salubrious circumstance my visit to Oxford coincided with perhaps its most critical and momentous bacchanalia, also redolent for me. Every first of May for hundreds of years, the choristers of Magdalen have sung carols and lavish madrigals in Latin at dawn from the top of the college tower. In the strenuously bilious Oxford setting, May Morning occasions a traditional drinking fete that begins the previous evening and intensifies with the coming of the light. The pubs open at six-thirty a.m., and even in Oxford, epitome for many of ponderous dignity, there is dancing in the streets.

For the voyeuristic observer it began at eight p.m. of May Morning Eve in the grand sedate dining room of the Randolph Hotel, that paradigm of Empire in its apogee. Dominating the dining room were an enormous portrait of the first duke of Buckingham and the gilded crests of the Oxford colleges. One could only imagine the Randolph at the Victorian apex, but on this evening approaching another *fin de siècle* its ambience was rather mournful and sepulchral and bereft. There was a mere scattering of diners, sartorially proper. They were communicating in whispers. The waiters whispered too, but more regally.

I had requested a table beside a bay window with a good vista of the thoroughfare approaching Saint Giles. Outside the window was an Oxford tableau not in the least unfamiliar to me. Across the thoroughfare was the severe gray Gothic outback of Balliol College. To our left was the looming hulk of the Martyrs' Memorial, near the spots on which Cranmer, Latimer, and Ridley were burned at the stake in the 1550s, and to the right the ancient graveyard of Saint Mary Magdalen Church with its rows of mossy stones to the medieval dead, and adjacent to it a lighted telephone booth with people queued up to use it, and a few yards from this a beautiful twin-trunked elm only half in bloom. The bustle of vehicular traffic would have done justice to the Long Island Expressway on a Friday afternoon. A long narrow van came by with "Dial-a-Curry" in block letters on its doors, and red double-decker buses, and motorcycles, and dozens of bicycles, and a solitary black Rolls-Royce with a shadowy turbaned figure in the back seat.

Against this piebald backdrop, just as the bell in Tom Tower of Christ Church began its 101 nightly chimes, the hastening pedestrians on the sidewalk suddenly seemed to have mightily increased, all heading toward some arcane destination having to do with May Morning Eve. Pakistanis in bus-conductor suits, Bengalis in white trousers, Jamaicans in faded blue jeans, working-class maidens smoking Woodbines, Cowley factory lads in frayed leather jackets, and then hundreds of young collegiate gentlemen in tuxedos carrying bottles of champagne and university girls in smart identical black suits with tight-fitting miniskirts—all rushing toward their appointment, not the least, it seemed at the moment, in celebration, but with a nearly rank and churlish resolve. Later, as we departed the Randolph, we sighted the collegians up the street, gathered in huge concentric clusters, drinking champagne from the bottle, while the Pakistanis and Bengalis and Jamaicans and working-class fledglings silently observed them, and a threadbare ensemble of a half-dozen nonconformists disapprovingly sang an a cappella "Jesus Christ Will Rise Again."

Along toward midnight, not long after the pubs closed, from our hostelry on Saint Michael's lane we glanced out our window onto the courtyard of the Oxford Union's Victorian quarters, the university debating society, whose most famous resolution had been the 1933 one declaring its members "will in no circumstances fight for its King and country." There, fifteen or twenty future prime ministers, Chancellors of the Exchequer, and High Commissioners drank from tall mugs and argued among themselves in querulous high-pitched voices; they seemed ready to fight anyone now. In lodgings all down the street drunk students bickered, shouted, sang, engaged in specious soliloquies that trailed off unresolved, and then in the middle of the lane approached a cadre of loud, tipsy young men in their tuxedos, their footfalls heavy in the fog, as if apparitions were howling out at me. They were shouting: "On, Eton!" I raised the window and shouted back: "To hell with Etonians and Texas Aggies!" They looked up, uncomprehending of the import of this manifesto, I sensed, and then proceeded vociferously into the night.

Dawn came in the raw gloom. Under the magnificent Magdalen Tower with its high, benign pinnacles, the previous evening's scene unfolded once more. The disheveled students in tuxedos and miniskirts, one youngster's trousers ripped open from ankle to waist, were still drinking from their champagne bottles, and town chaps and their glassy-eyed escorts from their Woodpecker Cider magnums—a social amalgam across the divide—and below the Magdalen Bridge the river was lined with punts, and from an arched Gothic roof above a queue of gargoyles, three or four Magdalen men poured champagne down upon the crowd, all of it reminding me of nothing if not an Ole Miss–Mississippi State football game, or an Oklahoma-Texas. Sitting on a nearby street curb, several students were singing one of their popular tunes: *If you don't know me by now/You will never, never, never know me. . . .*

Then, in a moment, all was hushed. The bells rang, and from the great, serene tower etched against the melancholy dawn the Latin hymn wafted out above the celebrative young, suddenly stilled, and floated across the tiny green river, and gently over the spires and meadows of the haunted old town, as if the town might be saying in solicitude: "We have seen all this before." In that instant, precisely thirty-four years ago to the awakening hour, my comrades and our English girls were launching our punts northward on this river, champagne in hand, for a miniature river island named Mesopotamia, where we stayed till dark and got gloriously drunk. It was, after all, May Morning, and time was passing, and, like ourselves, also merely mortal.

JoAnne and I were dining the first evening of my return at an Indian restaurant on the High. Nearby at a lengthy table were a dozen or so students. The brilliant Oxford banter, the half-studied and mildly cynical badinage, will likely never change. The difference was boys and girls together. In my era women were restricted to their own colleges. Today only two of the colleges, and these women's ones, are segregated by sex. The Oxford misogyny was notorious. Until a century ago, college dons could not marry. Degrees for women were allowed only as recently as 1920. Now women have roughly a third of the places at Oxford. And a substantial number of the American Rhodes Scholarships, all-male until 1976, go to women.

Hand-holding was unusual a generation ago. In that regard now, Oxford could be Ann Arbor; it is mellowing. Dress codes also appear to have relaxed. Oxonians now dress more like their American counterparts. As with other pockets of Britain, it is more like the United States, for better or worse, because of the increased Americanization of England and, conversely, because of the heightened internationalization of many places in the United States. By the same token, contemporary Oxford has a more European flavor than before. British entry into the Common Market has surely had an effect. Oxford has always been of the world, but the European overtones are more pronounced than they ever were. Foreign tongues are heard in more abundance. A pub I often frequented on North Parade was a hushed, morbid little spot. Today it is dazzlingly modern, with a blackboard announcing lasagna, chili, Mediterranean pizza, and Hawaiian ham and cheese, and many of its patrons are European.

Although much of its suburbia is incomparably drab, and working-class neighborhoods remain sadly bleak, the look of much of Oxford is more affluent. The food is better. The pubs sell Jack Daniel's, which may suggest something. Yet, there is a price to be paid for Americans. The deterioration of the dollar since my student time is ghastly and embarrassing; it has lost close to seventy-five percent of its former authority. A pint of bitter in an Oxford pub is an unerring gauge. One pint cost a half-crown, thirty cents, in the late 1950s, today more than $2.

Oxford around the business thoroughfare of Cornmarket has incorporated the most catastrophic textures of America—misbegotten supermarkets, chain stores, Burger Kings, McDonald's, Kentucky Fried, all within proximity of ancient churches and colleges. Near the Crown Inn, where Shakespeare often stayed, the Golden Cross Inn off Cornmarket, dating to 1200, with its medieval courtyard and oriel windows, displays a sign declaring it specializes in Pizza Express. In the university itself, on my casual surmise—clothes, accents, and yes, a certain classically audacious demeanor—the rich, privileged youth from the great private schools (in England private schools are actually called public schools) seem to dominate, and sly legacies of Edwardian grandeur survive in one or another form everywhere. But if the facts be known, the ratio for more than a generation now of undergraduates on state scholarships or public grants has been roughly two-to-one. Yet, as Jan Morris has truthfully measured it, this is a university "still on its own, still half aloof to change. It has tried to adapt an aristocratic tradition to an egalitarian age, and though to the sympathetic observer this generally looks admirable, if a little forlorn, to the critic it is often simply arrogant." And the returning son can only confirm Jan Morris's perception that the undergraduates themselves seem not to have altered in any tangible dimension, much as one is tempted to look for it:

"The social proportions have shifted, but the same classic figures stroll these quadrangles. Here is the poor Welsh scholar, black-haired and dis-approving, and here is the Duke's son on his way to dinner at the Grid-iron Club: the ambitious still stalk contemptuously among the frivolities, the heedless still race up to London with lovely girls in powerful sports cars. . . . Many undergraduates still look, as they always have, unmistak-ably degenerate, and for all the economic revolution many still manage to throw excellent champagne-parties in college rooms on summer eve-nings."

Rather, of course, it is those of us who have departed it who have changed.

One arrives upon the Turf Tavern, *my* pub, through a maze of medie-val alleys, bordered by tall, half-timbered lodgings. It is situated unpre-possessingly at the end of a widening cobbled lane only a few yards from a gaunt stone wall of New College. It was a small yet shambling medieval establishment much like the one described by Thomas Hardy in *Jude the Obscure;* I believe Hardy was secretly infatuated with his own character, Arabella the barmaid. In my day it was a muted, mellow little sanctuary, presided over by an elderly brother and sister, whose ugly yellow cat sometimes perched on our table as we took our infinite pints of bitter. Is the yellow cat who greets us at the door on this day a great-great-grandson?

The fine old Turf is largely gone. Enterprising new owners have made of it a short-order establishment with video games and piercing music. I could have collapsed in my tracks of a sundered heart. Yet the contours of the interior rooms are not dissimilar, and the beer garden in back is not uninviting, and the warm, resonant English ale with which JoAnne in our days here has become against all expectations smitten, is still lyrical to the spirits.

A pretty undergraduate girl, carrying a cello in a leather case twice as big as she, enters the door, deposits the cello in a corner, and sits at the adjoining table. Instinctually I know that the young men and women seated there are from New College down the way. They are consuming great quantities of beer, and I am eavesdropping. A rather dogmatic young man is lecturing three young women, including the late arrival, on sexual mores in the United States. He explains he has spent a recent vacation there. "In America sex is A to zed rather than A to B," he is saying. "The alternatives are endless and self-perpetuating, actually. American life is so vital, so charged and full of life. It's horrendously more complicated than it appears from here. You must go." The girls nod in genial assent. One of them will spend the summer at Vassar.

It could have been a dialogue at that very table straight out of 1957, an Oxonian having just returned from the States in a proselytizing humor, the same words, gestures, intonations, caught for me in a frieze of *déjà vu.*

"Were you ever so young?" JoAnne whispers. "I know you were. I've seen pictures."

With the wretched reminder, I knew it was time to go back at last to my old college. For, in truth, I had been postponing it.

The approach to the college is from Catte Street with its gauntlet of university buildings, the Bodleian, the Clarendon, the Sheldonian Theatre, the Radcliffe Camera, down a tortuous passage called New College Lane, which Max Beerbohm called "a grim ravine." New College was new in 1379. It was founded by one William of Wykeham, Bishop of Winchester, to ameliorate the ravages to the clergy of the Black Death, and to produce "men of good learning, fruitful to the Church of God and to the King and Realm." How did an American boy fit into *that?*

In Oxford, you belong to your college by right forever. This was not the visiting hour, and a stern front-lodge porter challenged me just inside the gateway. "I'm a member of the college." He was all charm in a twinkling. "Welcome back, sir. You'll find things changed. We have ladies now, sir. It complicates matters." Was Thompson still here? "Who, sir?" My old scout, Thompson. "Oh, no sir. He's gone these many years." The dons of my day: most of them dead or retired. I turned to enter the old precincts. "You will fetch me if you need anything, won't you, sir?"

And suddenly, there it was, the fine sweep of the Great Quad in its fourteenth-century grandeur, its oval lawn as manicured as a golf green, its stringent staircases and passageways, precisely as I had departed it thirty years ago, catching the day's declining sun now all tawny gray and gold.

As I wandered the college in that hour before twilight, its little mysterious alcoves and cul-de-sacs leapt out in buried recognition. From students' rooms came the sounds of a piano, a saxophone, a violin, giving way now to the echoes of the boys' choir in Evensong from the chapel.

The concrete stairs leading to the dining hall were deeply grooved with the footsteps of the two-score generations. In the medieval hall itself, empty now, where we dined on kipper and oatmeal at breakfast, and vintage roast beef and potatoes the rest of the time, the same portraits of warriors and ecclesiastics and parliamentarians still gazed gloomily down on the long dark tables; at one of them a young Englishman once asked me to describe the precise odor of a skunk, and the physiognomy of armadillos, and whether rattlesnakes could bite through boots. And then through magisterial wrought-iron gates into the luxuriant recess of the college gardens, the most beautiful in Oxford bordered by the twelfth-century Old City Wall, and with the same overgrown and profligate eighteenth-century mound right in the middle. At the farthest turn of the gardens I looked back and saw the entity of the college itself, a citadel in the soft, orange light.

It was only instinct that led me through a murky, winding little alleyway, moribund as it always was in its enveloping dark, into my own quadrangle—and momentarily I was standing at the window of my old rooms. It was only a sham: Had it been thirty-five years since I dwelled here? Surely it was merely a fortnight ago. The Old City Wall! I had seen it from my worktable here in the mists of that first autumn, in the dark of winter when the sun always set so early there hardly seemed a day at all, and now on this fading spring afternoon I gazed again on those gray bastions and turrets and sentries' walks eight centuries old. All around me in the college now, as then, were the sounds of summer term: the boys' choir in the chapel, a violin and a flute from the room down the way, a popular tune from a radio, the shouts of the cricketers headed back from the parks by the Cherwell. The only difference was the presence of the girls, strolling the lawns together, or with the boys. The air was dizzy with the blossoms and the flowering trees and the miraculous green. Had I ever really left it at all?

Sitting here alone so many hours each day with this perspective before me, and with my stacks of history books, I remember as vividly as yesterday how awhirl was my brain with the falterings of civilization, and my own secret view of the human race as masses in flight or in rapine, biblical swarms fleeing ruin or wreaking it, always trying to survive, or to destroy. Yet this timeless beauty from my window always mocked my dismal theory, just as it mocked me now.

Everywhere were the whimsical ghosts of youth. There were five of us first-year Yanks here, and we all lived around this quadrangle, and at any instant I half expected one of them to emerge in loping American gait from the passageway and shout across the greensward to me: "Where have *you* been?" But where were *they?* Biographical fact will not, I think, suffice: Rudenstine of Princeton, now president of Harvard; Suddarth of Yale, former ambassador to Jordan; Ooms of Amherst, a prominent Washington economic advisor; D'Arms of Princeton, graduate dean at Michigan. None of this will do, for they belong here now.

The porters locked the gates to the college at eleven back then, securing them with padlocks and iron, and the only way to get in, or out for that matter, was to climb a treacherous stone salient behind the library, over spikes and broken glass embedded in the stone, and even the nimble, athletic Ooms once suffered a nasty gash from the spikes one nocturnal climb. Locked inside, we peregrinated these monastic confines in the late hours. A mystic from New Delhi with obscure eyes claimed to communicate with the college spirits. I once ran into him in the gardens at two a.m. kneeling in the grass, his arms spread to the heavens in supplication; I got away from there fast.

In the farther corner of this quadrangle, on a luminous June day of '57, as a mucilaginous band of tourists watched in disbelief, we used a Coca-Cola bottle to christen a 1934 Buick touring car we had purchased for fifty pounds to take us to Rome. We had christened it "Foster," after John Foster Dulles, but Foster did not even make it to Dover. On this swathe of quadrangle lawn, Rudenstine once hit me fly balls with my own baseball bat and ball. Using the Old City Wall as an outfield fence, I patrolled it against his audacious flies and drives. He dispatched a long, towering fly that barely missed the stained-glass windows of the chapel. "That's it!" Rudenstine yelled petulantly. "That's the last time I'll do this!" And the future president of Harvard retired to his essay paper on Roman Britain and the threat to it of the Picts and Scots.

And not just the Yanks, but the English, too. Where are you, Palmer,

Cocks, Black, Potter, Briarly, Hugh-Jones? In this smoky New College dusk I need your dexterous bon mots and full-blooded lunacies.

My last stop, I know, will be the cloisters, a damp hidden quarter with an enormous oak in a corner, as I remembered it, planted there, we were told, by the druids, and under which once loitered, inexplicably, a giant 300-year-old turtle. What could a 300-year-old turtle *do* but loiter? I look now for this singular creature but cannot find him. Do even ancient turtles die in New College? All about me, on the floors and walls, are the memorials to the dead, and on the bell tower above the mad carvings of the gargoyles. I have never been able to put these grotesqueries out of my mind. They are smiling, laughing, crying, grimacing, staring outward in abject terror, biting their fingers, as if making jest of real humanity in its inexpressible foible, and in its passing. Who created these funny monsters, I always wondered, and what on earth do they mean?

In the cloistral hush I indulgently reflect on all that has transpired with one in the thirty years he has been away from this place: the successes, the failures, the joys and the sorrows, the loves and the friendships come and gone, the catastrophic whims and transmutations. The young boys of the college choir I once saw from my window marching double-file each day through the quadrangle to the chapel, predecessors to the choristers now singing their final Latin psalm at Evensong up the way, are not forty years old! I have not forgotten how much I loved this place, and feared it, and the fear and awe and ambivalence come back to me now, that they might yet inhibit or consume me. And as for this, my college, circa 1379, how much has *it* changed? Many generations have passed through here. What are thirty years, indeed, to six hundred?

In these days' wanderings, the direst of recognitions began to spring in my poor psyche that I had not made the slightest ripple on this indwelling place, for Oxford somehow obliterates you, and especially the American. Robert Penn Warren, who was two years here, confessed to me a long time ago that he did not get a single poem out of it. Yet I conceded, too, that I had once dwelled here, and that the old town had imbued me in my youth with . . . *something*. And perhaps that is enough.

Just before leaving I indulged myself in a spiritual pilgrimage to Castell's, the varsity shop in the Broad, to buy an official Half-Blue tie.

This is the Oxford equivalent of an American varsity letter jacket, and I had won it years ago, not for cricket or rugby or crew, but for basketball, on the Oxford University team that had won the national championship. I had come across my Half-Blue tie not long before this return to Oxford, in a box containing the mementos of those years—tutorial essays written in a young man's prose, the menu of a Commemoration Ball, the tassel from my mortarboard, yellowed invitations to sherries and teas, my diploma, faded photographs catching the revelry of a fine May afternoon, the baseball we almost broke the stained-glass windows with. The old blue-and-white tie was worn and mildewed, the blue nearly faded away, the white a sickly gray. With a ceremonious gesture I had thrown it in the garbage. But now I wished a new one, wanted some fragment of myself to carry home. "Oxford varsity, sir?" the Castell's clerk inquired. "Yes, indeed." I replied. "Then welcome back!" he said.

On the last day of our stay, JoAnne and I bought a big carton of a dozen or so jars of Oxford Original Marmalade at Frank Cooper's, in the High, to take to friends back home. We were walking down New College lane toward the hotel to collect our luggage. Momentarily we were again in front of my old college. I was tempted to visit it one final time before leaving it forever, to bid it farewell for the last time in my life, but the marmalade was heavy, and I knew it really was time to go.

I had had a bizarre, shadowy dream the night before. Eudora Welty, Truman Capote, Shelby Foote, my mother, and a saturnine figure I took to be William of Wykeham were sitting in the Turf Tavern admonishing me in Latin to do right, and to beware of the rascals. Is that what Oxford was saying to me?

"Nostalgia isn't what it used to be," Peter deVries observed. At first I thought this modest pilgrimage would be about growing older, about youth lost, but I see now it is really about the complexity of remembrance. What I was looking for all the time was me, and I was not there.

Coming on Back

The Day I Followed the Mayor around Town

(Editor's note: Willie Morris wrote the date "9/6/78" on his original copy of "The Day I Followed the Mayor around Town" and inscribed it to his son: "To David, a little whimsy of love and feeling at the beginning of your sophomore year. Never falter in what you care for. I love you—Daddy." Below the title and byline he typed: "To Marina, a little girl who has a lot of big dogs." The typescript of this previously unpublished essay is from the Willie Morris Collection, Department of Archives and Special Collections, John Davis Williams Library, University of Mississippi.)

I

I am acquainted with dogs. In Mississippi when I was a boy, I grew up with dogs. First there were the tall, slender bird dogs my father and I took hunting in the Delta swamps. They helped us hunt quail and squirrels, and they shared in the feasts my mother made from these delicacies of the forest. Their names were Tony, Sam, and Jimbo, and on those long-ago winter nights down in Yazoo when I was growing so fast that my knees and elbows hurt, Tony, Sam, and Jimbo slept in my bed with me, wrapping themselves around me soft as ermine, waking me every morning at two o'clock with their sudden howls as the Memphis-to-New Orleans train roared through the drowsing town. As the years passed, one by one my bird dogs died. I prayed they had all gone up to the Methodist dog heaven.

Then there was a succession of English smooth-haired fox terriers. Their names were Sonny, Duke, and finally Old Skip, shipped down to us all the way from a kennel in Missouri. Old Skip was the smartest dog in the state of Mississippi. I got him in the fourth grade and he went right through high school with me. He was black and white and had a sturdy body, and with the exception of Ichabod Crane, a dog of my adulthood, he was the most athletic of all my dogs. He could play football with the boys or catch a tennis ball thrown forty feet up on the fly. Every morning for years he walked the eight blocks to school with me, then went back home and lounged under an elm tree all day until I returned. He loved listening to the radio, especially country music, and he went to Mr. Buddy Reeves's grocery store every morning to fetch the *Memphis Commercial Appeal* for us, returning with it rolled up in his mouth. We were inseparable in the summers of my youth, in that isolated southern hamlet before the expressways and television, and I can see his funny black face as if the years had stood still for me.

I taught Old Skip how to drive a car. I would prop him on the steering wheel of my father's green DeSoto and duck my head under the dashboard. We would drop by the Dew Drop Inn where the old Negro men sat on their haunches in front, chewing tobacco and whittling on wood amidst the dusty facades. With my foot on the accelerator I would slow the car to ten or twelve miles an hour and guide the steering wheel with a couple of fingers. Old Skip would have the steering wheel in his paws, his long black head peering through the windshield at the dirt road ahead. The men would shout: "Look at that old dog drivin' a car!" Old Skip, the comrade of my adolescence, died when I was far away in college, trying to outflank a flea which had plagued him for most of a decade. My father buried him in the backyard not far from Tony, Sam, Jimbo, Sonny, and Duke.

2

Years later, when I was a grown man living in New York, I got my little boy David a fox terrier like Old Skip. She was a girl and we named her Harper. One night David saw her killed by a car in front of our farmhouse. He grieved as only little boys can grieve. He vowed he would never again have another dog.

The days passed. On misty evenings I read to the little boy from Washington Irving, a writer of brooding and scary tales who had lived not far from us many years before. I especially read to him *The Legend of Sleepy Hollow*, and his eyes grew wide as he heard about the Dutch schoolteacher frightened away by the Headless Horseman. Slow as could be, in that strange chemistry of diminishing hurt, he began to change his mind. All of a sudden one day he said that he wanted a big dog who would fit the name "Ichabod Crane."

He and I searched many counties in the Hudson River Valley. This quest lasted for weeks. We followed the classified advertisements in the newspapers. We visited kennels and looked at German shepherds, Dalmatians, collies, Irish setters, sheepdogs, bulldogs, and various other kinds of outstanding puppies. But the little boy always looked at them and shook his head. They failed to fit the name.

We had almost given up. Then one luminous autumn afternoon, the fields of the Hudson Valley lush with corn and pumpkins sometimes far as the eye could see, we drove a long way to look at some black Labrador retrievers. The owner of the kennel opened the gate to a fence and six shiny black puppies came out, wobbling back and forth on their new legs. One of them circled around for a while, investigated a shrub with much curiosity, and then came to David, nuzzling his hand with a cold, wet nose. David sat down to touch him. Then he looked up at me. "That's him," he said. "That's Ichabod Crane."

We wrapped him in a blanket and took him home, and he was with us for seven years, our Ichabod Crane. He grew so fast he almost buzzed like a bee, and when he reached his full size, he was coal black and strong, with floppy ears and web feet and liquid brown eyes full of comprehension. He was a fount of delight and unfailing mischief, a devilish intellect, a retriever of sticks, balls, and all other flying objects, a loyal friend of tenderness and love. He slept in the bed with David as my old bird dogs had done, but he never once howled at the trains. When we moved to a small village on Long Island called Bridgehampton, we found him to be an ocean swimmer, too, and we would watch his head bobbing above the Atlantic waves on many afternoons of summer.

We were planning a beach cookout for Ichabod Crane on his seventh birthday. But that day he did not come home. David and I got in the car and drove around the countryside for hours. On a road near the ocean I saw a black speck far in the distance, and as we drove closer it was the unfolding of my deepest premonitions. It was Ichabod Crane, struck dead by a car. David and I put him gently in the back seat and went home and cried. Later we buried him in one of his favorite places, under some shade trees by a cool inland pond.

The little boy was no longer so little and the father was no longer so young. It was the father this time who vowed never to have another dog.

3

The island seasons changed and changed again. The years passed, and the little boy went away to college.

There was a dog I had begun to notice casually in the village, a black Labrador almost the replica of Ichabod Crane, about the same age and with the same floppy ears and black mane and liquid brown eyes, yet more pensive in his demeanor—a pedigreed individual, for sure, with good blood flowing in his veins, yet with scars here and there on his body from his wanderings of the earth. He had come to the village from Lord knows where, and he more or less lived with the men who ran the service station on Main Street. Had he run away from some cruel master somewhere? Or had he simply sought out our village as a fine place to settle down? No one knew, but after a time the questions which at first intrigued everyone did not matter at all. Since I would stop at the service station for gasoline, I got to know this most distinguished vagabond whose name was Pete. Sometimes I would bring bits of candy to him, and he grew to recognize my car and would hail me down on Main Street and ask to ride around with me for a while. He would get in the back seat and stick his head out the window to let the breeze rustle his big old ears. Or he would sit up front with me to let me know he liked me. When he took a nap in the village, it was in the shade of the war memorial with the names on it of the village boys killed in all the wars. He got to know everyone in town and would wander up and down Main Street all day greeting the people. It was for just such as this that Pete came to be known as "The Mayor of Bridgehampton." Once David, back home on a vacation, took a photograph of Pete at the war memorial and had it published in the local newspaper, which ran it with the caption: "His Honor the Mayor."

Then an unexpected thing happened. One afternoon I heard a loud scratching at my back door and went to see who it was. It was Pete, asking to be let inside. I opened the door and he came right in and flopped down next to the sofa, as if he owned the place. He stayed there most of the day. Around sunset I told him to get back to the service station before it closed. He refused to leave.

I had often talked to the dogs I knew, particularly when they were being unreasonable, so I said: "Look, Mr. Mayor, I promised myself I wouldn't ever have another dog." When he looked up at me, I was certain he understood. But he did not budge.

Pete had come to live with me. I was convinced, in fact, that for the past several weeks he had been looking me over with just that aim in mind. Had he been a human, he would have brought along a toothbrush and a suitcase; it was that kind of decision.

So now I have another dog, and a most unlikely one he is. Unlike Ichabod Crane, he refuses to chase sticks or balls. When I throw something for him, he simply gazes at me as if such diversions are beneath his official station. Furthermore, he is the only Labrador I ever saw who does not like the water. He will go to the beach and stroll down to the ocean and put his paw in it and then grimace with distaste. As with Old Skip, I tried to teach him to drive a car, but he spurned that also. I am not suggesting that he is lazy; it is merely that he has certain priorities. He moves slowly, with a studied calm that borders on a royal dignity. He is not young—Doctor Gould, the veterinarian, once looked down in his mouth and ears and pronounced him to be eight years old—but his age has nothing to do with these circumscriptions. It finally dawned on me that Pete knows he is the Mayor.

It is for this reason, among others, that he is the most fiercely independent dog I ever knew, zealously aware of his own prerogatives, a living symbol of Jeffersonian democracy. He goes his own way whenever he wishes; most of the day he is in the village among his constituents.

Sometimes I believe he considers me slightly insane. He sleeps under the worktable where I write, and occasionally he wakes up and looks at me at work on my typewriter, as if to say: "Why do you pound on that little box all day, you crazy fool?" In retaliation, occasionally I pick the ticks off him one by one.

Yet, since I am acquainted with dogs, I know that beneath our alliance lies an ineffable friendship. The gestures of it are not idle. When he sights me in the village in his eternal peregrinations, he rushes up to me with his eyes ablaze and embraces me with his paws. When I talk to him as he lies on the floor of our house, his tail thuds vigorously on the floor with the sound of each word. Sometimes he nuzzles my hand with his nose, just as Ichabod Crane did many years ago when David discovered him at the kennel in the Hudson Valley, and he says to me with his eyes: "Good ol' buddy."

4

One morning quite recently I decided to follow him into the village without his knowing it, merely to see what he does with his rugged independence. He breakfasted on half a can of dog food, then left the house at 10:00 A.M. as he always does and strolled down the broad boulevard dappled in the shade of enormous oak trees toward Main Street. I gave him a decent start, then trailed surreptitiously fifty yards behind him.

His first stop was in front of the Polish grocery, where he greeted the old men who loiter there at all hours. "There's the Mayor!" one of them shouted, and the others swiftly joined in the chorus. Pete made his salutations to each person, then sat among them for a while watching the cars go by. A large dog named Cato, known in the village as Pete's police commissioner, appeared from around a corner and sat next to Pete scanning the morning scene—a kind of informal policy conference, perhaps. I was hiding behind the war memorial and watched Pete as he got up and crossed the street to the drug store, pushed open the door with his nose, and walked inside to see Emil, the proprietor. "Good morning, Your Honor," I heard Emil say, and Pete sniffed among the cosmetics and waited around tactfully until Emil gave him a LifeSaver mint.

After a few minutes he strolled outside again and went next door to the library. He sat on the front lawn as the people he knew came by, each one calling him by name, paying their deferences to the dignity of his office. Next he ambled down to the Village Restaurant, opened the door again with his nose, and went in to mingle with the potato farmers having their morning coffee. "Hello, Mr. Mayor!" I heard a shout from inside. "How's politics today?"

After ten minutes or so with the potato farmers, he emerged once more. I trailed at a discreet distance as he paused near the hardware store and played a while with some small children, then said hello to the people waiting in line at the welfare office. Momentarily he pushed his way into the Vogue Beauty Salon and dallied for an interval with the ladies reading the Hollywood magazines under the hair driers. Next he went to the bank to see the tellers and the people he knew cashing checks. After that he walked down to the post office and tarried among the activity there, then he went to each of the three bars in the village to give his respects to the morning beer drinkers. In the bars there was much amiable banter directed his way, and one solicitation in particular: "Here's our Mayor! How about a Budweiser, Your Honor?"

Next, as I hid behind a tree near the Community House, he stopped at the Candy Kitchen to welcome the high school students at their noontime break; one of them rubbed his back and presented him the remnants of an ice cream cone. Then on to the jailhouse, where he poised beneath a cell window and a prisoner he had gotten to know threw him a piece of bread. His stop after this was the train station to see who might step off the 12:15 from Penn Station. He only recognized one person here, an elderly gentleman named Halsey who paused to give his ears a friendly tug.

Then he retraced his steps back up Main Street, moving ever so slowly, stopping to exchange salutations with his constituents on the sidewalk. Sometimes he wandered onto the porches of the houses lining the street to pass a little time with the women sweeping or snapping string beans. Near the church with its tall spire gleaming in the sunshine he loitered with some construction workers who were putting in a new sewer; he stood at the edge of the hole in the street and gazed into it with official curiosity. He glowered at a pair of frolicsome cats—a stare of cold political hostility—and as I spied on him from behind a large gravestone, he lay down with all four feet sticking up and scratched his back vigorously on the grass. Occasionally someone in a passing car would see him and yell: "Hi there, Pete! How's His Honor today?"

Fully rested after a few minutes, he got up, stretched and yawned, and looked up and down Main Street again. Since nothing unusual caught his attention, he took a short cut through the graveyard and several backyards to our house. Knowing him as I did, he would now have an afternoon siesta and then, regular as a metronome, repeat his morning ritual later in the day, stopping at the places he had not had the inclination to visit on his earlier rounds.

He is sleeping now under my worktable. I look down at him, awash in his Labrador dreams. Once I thought he might be Ichabod Crane, returned from the grave to watch out for me. No—he is too much his own character for such as that. He is Pete and nobody else. Yet he brings back to me my boyhood, all the long-ago things I miss—my father's footsteps on the porch, my mother playing a hymn on the piano, all the boys and girls I once knew, and the smells of a new spring morning in Mississippi. And in him for me are the vanished spirits of Tony, Sam, Jimbo, Sonny, Duke, and Old Skip—especially good Old Skip dead these years. Dogs give continuity to a man's life; they help hold the fractured pieces of it together. When Pete the Mayor came to live with me, he reaffirmed the contours of my own existence.

Coming on Back

My people settled and founded Mississippi—warriors and politicians and editors—and I was born and raised into it, growing up in a town, half delta and half hills, before the television culture and the new Dixie suburbia, absorbing mindlessly the brooding physical beauty of the land, going straight through all of school with the same white boys and girls. We were touched implicitly, even without knowing it, with the schizophrenia of race and imbued in the deep way in which feeling becomes stronger than thought with the tacit acceptance that Mississippi was different, with a more profound inwardness and impetuosity and a darker past not just than that of New York, or Ohio, or California, but of Arkansas, Tennessee, Alabama and Louisiana, which were next door. This was a long time before anyone deigned to think that a southerner could be elected President of the United States with everything that this would imply—not only elected in large measure with southern votes but, four years later, turned out resoundingly with southern votes as well.

I went away to college in Texas, and in England, and ran a newspaper in Texas, and sojourned in California, and edited a national magazine in New York City and, having served my time in our cultural capital as many of us must, moved out to the eastern tip of Long Island to a village by the sea.

I did not know then that I was an exile, almost in the European sense. When I met a fellow Mississippian by chance, the exchange of tales about family and places, the stories about football or fishing or some long-vanished preacher were signs of a strange mutuality. I would meet black Mississippians in the North who were more similar to me in background and preferences than the Yankee WASPs I saw every day.

One somber twilight I stood at the corner of Lexington and Forty-Ninth waiting for the light to change. Suddenly a woman appeared from the anonymous manswarm and began hitting me about the shoulders and head with her umbrella. "You beast!" she shouted. "You almost let me get hit by that taxicab." "Madame," I wished to say, "I didn't see it either," but the blows continued to descend, and I retreated into the doorway of a Nedick's. As I stood there, I seemed to hear the long resonant echo of the noon whistle from down by the river in the drowsing summers of home, confessing somehow to myself that I may have taken on more than I had bargained for.

I often dwell on the homecomings I have made—the acutely physical sensations of returning from somewhere else to all those disparate places I have lived. To the town of my childhood—Yazoo—it was the precarious hills looming like a mountain range at the apex of that triangle known as the Mississippi Delta, the lights of the town twinkling down at night in a diaphanous fog. To the city of my college days—Austin—it was the twin eminences of the University Tower and the grand old State Capitol awash in light from very far away. To the citadel of my young adulthood—Oxford University—it was the pallid sunlight catching all in filigree the spires and cupolas of that medieval city on the Thames. To the metropolis of my ambition it was the Manhattan skyline that seemed so forbidding yet was at once so compact and close at hand. To the village of my gentlest seclusion, on Long Island, it was the Shinnecock Canal opening onto that other world of shingled houses, flat potato fields and dunes, and the blue Atlantic breakers.

It was in the East that I grew to middle age. I cared for it, but it was not mine. I had lived nearly twenty years there, watching all the while from afar as my home suffered its agonies, loving and hating it across the distance, returning constantly on visits or assignments. The funerals kept apace, "Abide with Me" reverberating from the pipe organs of the churches, until one day I awoke to the comprehension that all my people were gone. As if in a dream, where every gesture is attenuated, it grew upon me that a man had best be coming on back to where his strongest feelings lay.

The remarkable literary tradition of Mississippi derives from the complexity of a society that still, well into the late twentieth century, retains much of its communal origins, and along with that a sense of continuity, of the enduring past and the flow of the generations—an awareness, if you will, of human history.

My friend William Styron, the novelist, recently came to visit, and on our drives through the countryside he said Mississippi reminded him of Russia—the sweep of sky above the forlorn hamlets, the interminable spaces, the burden of its history in its misery and loss, the pride of the people. Since my return, I myself have often felt an ineluctable similarity with Ireland—in the spoken and written language, the telling of tales, the mischief and eccentricity of the imagination, the guilts and blunderings and angers, the admiration of the hoax and fondness for strong drink, the relish of company and of idiosyncrasy for its own sake, the radiance and fire in the midst of impoverishment. These are qualities, I would discover, which still bounteously exist.

"Time is very important to us because it has dealt with us," Mississippi's Eudora Welty says. "We have suffered and learned and progressed through it." Many of the people I know here of my age had great-grandfathers and great-uncles who fought in the Civil War. Some survived it, some did not, having fallen at Brice's Cross Roads or Shiloh or Chancellorsville or Gettysburg in that near obliteration of the young officer class that rivaled the slaughter of a generation for England, France and Germany in World War I. The experiences of these men have been brought to their great-grandsons and -daughters through diaries found in attics, through the words handed down, and through the ancestral relics: a pistol, a sword, old buttons, a shred of gray cloth.

Many Americans, to express it boldly, are afraid of Mississippi. I witnessed this fear time and again in the East, and I see it to this day. It was, after all, not too many years ago that D. W. Brogan, who was a British historian but might just as well have been speaking for much of northern sentiment, could describe Mississippi as the most savage and backward of the then forty-eight American commonwealths. The Freedom Summer of 1964, when hundreds of northerners confronted here the intransigence of the police, the poverty and the cruelty, and went home with stories to tell, was only seventeen years ago. Only nineteen years have passed since President Kennedy sent 23,000 federal troops to Ole Miss to ensure the admission of its first black student, James Meredith, when Governor Ross

Barnett declared: "I refuse to allow this nigra to enter our state university, but I say so politely."

Mississippi's most horrific specters have always been racism and poverty. My friend Ed Perry, chairman of the appropriations committee of the state House of Representatives, complains over beer in the Gin Saloon in Oxford of the lack of funds for many essential services. "There's no money!" he shouts. "We have to juggle. There just ain't no money." He recalls what his grandfather, who was a farmer down in the hard land of Choctaw County, once told him: "Mississippi was the last state the Depression hit. Hell, we had a depression long before the Depression. People were so poor they didn't even know they were in one." The latest statistics reveal Mississippi to be so entrenched in fiftieth place in per capita income that it will likely never reach Arkansas in forty-ninth. The state consistently has the highest proportion of its people on food stamps, and much of the new industry brought down in recent years taps the reservoir of unemployment and easy labor by strictly adhering to the minimum wage.

The present governor warns that Mississippi is like "an emerging colonial nation" and must begin to be selective about the quality of industry brought into the state. In passionate words he warns, too, against the rampant economic growth that has already ruined large areas of the Deep South, and he deplores the pollution and indiscriminate dumping of hazardous wastes that have made many of the lakes and streams of my boyhood lifeless.

An acquaintance in Yazoo County writes me of the Big Black Swamp, where he has just been deer hunting. "I felt in a sacred spot," he says, "a kinship not only with my forebears, but with the land." His father and his uncle hunted there. So did his grandfather and great-grandfather and great-great-grandfather, the latter having come down here in the 1830s after the Choctaws had ceded their claim to the settlers. Now the Big Black woods are owned by big paper companies that lease out hunting rights. "Big Black Swamp has always been there," he laments, "a fixture, like the moon in the sky. When the paper companies feel they must 'harvest' their 'wood crop' there, will it become Big Black Parking Lot?"

The dilapidated shacks and the unpainted facades still abound, and although the paved streets and public housing in the older black sections of the towns seem prolific in contrast to the 1940s, a random drive through the rural areas or the larger cities reveals much of that same abject impoverishment, mainly black but white as well. Out in the delta, the very land itself seems bereaved with the countless half-collapsed, abandoned tenant shacks set against the copious delta horizon. These are testimonials to the largest mass exodus of a people in our history—the southern black migration northward since World War II. The triumph of Allis-Chalmers is everywhere, and the farm machinery companies pervade the landscape in such numbers as to astound one who remembers the numberless black silhouettes in these fields a generation ago, picking or chopping, pausing every so often to wave at the occasional car speeding by.

There are things here now that my grandfather, who was born shortly after the Civil War and who died in 1953, would find unfathomable. If he stepped out of his grave in the old section of the Raymond cemetery and came back to Jackson, I suspect the terrain along Interstate 55 with its mile upon mile of franchise establishments would astonish and frighten him. Modern-day Capitol Street and the Metrocenter Mall would leave him mystified, as would the traffic snarls and apartment complexes, the new suburbias, sprung full-born in all directions and not much different from the suburbs of Cincinnati or Denver.

Off the interstates and removed from the resounding nostrums of the New South lies our remembered world, the world of my childhood—old men in khakis whittling in the shade of a crossroads grocery; a domino game on the back stoop of a service station; an abandoned frame church with piles of used tires in front and a scrawled poster on top of them proclaiming, "Fried Chicken, Two Miles"; another sign at the chicken place itself, saying, "Roaches, Minnows, Worms and Hot Dogs"; a conversation between an ancient black man and woman in a store that serves also as the Trailways stop:

"How you doin' today, Annie?"

"Not too pretty good, but givin' thanks for bein' here."

In less than ten years, Mississippi and its sister states in the Deep South have undergone as fundamental a set of political changes as any in American history. The civil rights struggles of the 1960s were the catalyst, leading to two of the most crucial pieces of legislation ever passed by the United States Congress—the Civil Rights Act of 1964 and Voting Rights Act of 1965. All through the late 1960s and into the 1970s federal registrars arrived to help place black voters on the electoral rolls. Governor James K. Vardaman, running earlier in the century dressed in his white suit, white hat and white shoes in a white wagon driven by four white horses, seems a millenium away. The Democrats now appeal unabashedly for black support, emphasizing economic and educational concerns as a glue to their coalition. The Republicans also seek the black vote while mainly drawing on the young, rich whites of the courthouse squares and the suburbias. Mississippi, which ten years ago had the smallest number of registered black voters, now leads the nation in the number of elected black officials.

Much was brought to fruition last year in the election of William Winter as governor. Defeated in two earlier attempts when traditional segregationists joined forces against him, he was elected decisively this time. He is an eloquent student of history and literature. To use the words of Faulkner, he is not a Snopes, but a Sartoris. For years Winter has been the focus for those thousands of Mississippians who represented, in Lincoln's words, "the better angels of our nature"—he stood for racial moderation in the 1950s and 1960s when it was unpopular and even dangerous to do so.

When I was a boy, as they were wont to say in Mississippi, the only thing protecting Republicans was the game laws. Now, with two of the five U.S. congressmen and one of the state's U.S. senators, they are in an upsurge. Thad Cochran, forty-three, the senator who replaced James Eastland, was in the Ole Miss law school in 1962 during the Meredith episode. Along with William Winter, he is a symbol of Mississippi's ascent from bitterness and self-destruction, and he attracts a broad swath of support, including many progressive Democrats.

It is the proximity of Oxford and the Ole Miss campus, each populated by about 10,000 souls, that has given my homecoming its poignancy, for both have resonances of an older past. Youth and age are in healthy proportion, and the loyalty of the town to the university is both exuberant and touching. The courthouse in the middle of the square and the Lyceum at the crest of the wooded grove are little more than a mile apart, which is appropriate, for it is impossible to imagine Ole Miss in a big city, and Oxford without the campus would be another struggling northeast Mississippi town. One can drive around the campus and absorb the palpable sophistication of a small southern state university, and then proceed two or three miles into a countryside that is authentic boondocks upon which the twentieth century has only obliquely intruded.

Shortly after I came here, I was sitting on a sofa with Miss Louise, William Faulkner's sister-in-law. We were discussing the histories of some of the people buried in the cemetery. "It's an interesting town," she said. I told Miss Louise that I agreed. "It's so interesting," I replied, "I think somebody ought to write about it."

The presence of William Faulkner, the poet and chronicler of Mississippi, pervades this place, and living here has helped me know him better. His courage was of the Mississippi kind, and as with all great artists, he was a prophet on his own soil—about whites and blacks and the destruction of the land and the American Century and the human heart. W. H. Auden wrote on the death of William Butler Yeats, "Mad Ireland drove him to poetry," and Mississippi worked this way on Mr. Bill, for something moved in him when he finally decided to come back and write about the people and things he knew the best, creating his mythical land out of the real fibers of everything around him. Yet at the time he was laboring in solitude on much of the finest work an American ever wrote, he was deeply in debt, Ole Miss had little or nothing to do with him, and the town was baffled and perplexed by him. To many he was a failed and drunken eccentric.

Now William Faulkner is an industry in the town, ranking close to soybeans, timber, merchandising and Southeastern Conference football. Little clusters of Yankee and foreign tourists, including an unusual proportion of Japanese with their ubiquitous cameras, wander out to the grounds at Rowan Oak, or to St. Peter's Cemetery seeking his grave and those of his flamboyant kin, or search the back roads of Beat Two for modern-day Snopeses. Ole Miss conducts a sizable Faulkner seminar every summer and owns his wonderful old house set behind its magnolias and cedars, having won out over the University of Texas, which wished to dismantle the house and move Rowan Oak to a site near Austin, trees and all.

This reverence would no doubt bemuse Mr. Bill, but never mind. I find his spirit imperishable in the country people I see here, and in the old black men who sit on their haunches around the square and banter with the white merchants, and in the proudly individualistic storytellers of the town, and in the landmarks of his prose—the dank Yocona swamps and the slow-flowing rivers and the piny woods on a dreary winter's day.

In his corpus of fiction Faulkner wrote little about Ole Miss, although he had family antecedents there and he himself was briefly enrolled. He served as postmaster of the university post office until he was fired for not sorting the mail and for playing poker in the back with his friends, declaring after his dismissal that he was "sick and tired of being at the beck and call of every sonofabitch who could afford a two-cent stamp." In his stories he created Temple Drake, a genuine Ole Miss flapper of the Jazz Age, and a few campus scenes, but I suspect he wished to keep his mythical town and county more or less in its rude state, uncomplicated by such things as a university.

My dog Pete, less my dog than my brother, a big black Labrador of warmth and intelligence who once was the official mayor of Bridgehampton, Long Island, and still is, in absentia, likes the blending of the town of Oxford and the raw country that envelops it. We are a pair for lonely journeyings. Pete and I often visit St. Peter's cemetery to see Bill Appleton, the caretaker, and to talk with the gravediggers about the person who has just died on this day. Sometimes my friends come with us to show me the graves of their grandparents and great-grandparents.

Bill Appleton tells me about the foreign visitors who come to see Faulkner's grave. Sometimes they leave pints of bourbon at his tomb. Once I brought a New Orleans friend to St. Peter's, who talked at length with Bill, then asked him to explain why Mississippi has produced so many writers. "Because the hills around here are so poor and the farmin's no good," he said. "People ain't got nothin' else to do."

On the square one sees the people from their second-story windows, gazing down at the scenes of human commerce. One morning, walking in front of the Gumbo Company with the visiting writer, John Knowles, I said, "That's where we ate last night." An old man standing in front added: "And I bet it was mighty good too, wasn't it? Ain't it good to eat in there?" He then proceeded to talk with us about the virtue of soybeans over cotton and the steadfastness of mules.

Every native of this county, as in most of rural Mississippi, is still a hunter. The circumstances, however, are somewhat different from what they once were. Nowadays the hunting season in Lafayette County is a clear call for a four-wheel drive, 165-hp pickup, a high-powered automatic rifle with optional telescopic lens, CB radio, bourbon, and a good old boy's girlfriend if she is amenable.

They gather about the square before the light as they leave; they remind one a little of the Confederacy, although they are better equipped. A typical deer stand will be a friend's barn, with cows stirring at dawn, the good old boy relieving himself behind a haystack while his girlfriend, who came to town from Etta to work at the Ben Franklin selling cosmetics, with a natural predator's eye and a single 200-grain bullet, brings down a six-point buck who has been nibbling at the salt block. "Whew, I did it!" she says to her boyfriend on his return. It is her first kill, at least of deer.

CB radios announce the event from Hurricane to Toccopola. The sun is just breaking full over the misty landscape as trucks race from everywhere toward the scene. The word is out. "Ronni Sue—ol' Chick Field's girl—just got one out by Clear Creek!"

The Yoknapatawpha Press is a somewhat different expression of these Mississippi ironies and anomalies. The sole proprietor, editor, and janitor is Larry Wells, the husband of Faulkner's niece Dean Faulkner Wells. The office of his publishing company is located over the Sneed Ace Hardware Store on the square, and a contract with Wells is ritualized with a handshake in a saloon that was reconverted from a cotton gin rather than in the Sign of the Dove on Third Avenue, where such business is often done in Manhattan. Recently he brought out a reprint of a children's book I had once published in New York at the same time he published Dean's little volume recounting her uncle's ghost stories.

One night in the office above the hardware store, which had been Gavin Stevens's law office in the film *Intruder in the Dust*, I found myself with Dean and Larry putting dust jackets on books until the late hours, cutting the shrink-wrappage, and handling the telephone calls. At Dean's request I telephoned her house to see if her son "The Jaybird" was doing his homework. (He was watching television.) On a large crate of books Dean scrawled in a felt pen: "Packed and Written by the Author." Judy

Trott from Ole Miss and Patty Lewis from The Rose for Emily House dropped in to help. We gave them the shrink-wrappage. I told them I had never had such assignments from my various eastern publishers. "They don't do it this way at Random House," I said.

Observing all the old and new eccentricities within his purview, and contributing to them, is the mayor of Oxford, John Leslie, who reminds me in his verve of the Jewish mayor of Yazoo when I was growing up, although he does not get out and direct the Saturday night traffic as mayor Applebaum once did. John Leslie has been mayor for eight years, and was elected the year that beer was legalized in the town. "Hell," he says, "I beat beer by twenty-three votes."

Mayor Leslie is a big, cheerful soul of fifty-eight. Beneath the small-town Dixie facade, he is a man of courage and sensibility. He tries to get people to call him "Your Worship," as they address mayors in England, although the only constituent to do so is Faulkner's onetime bootleg-ger—a formidable country entrepreneur named Motee Daniels. The mayor presides over the town from behind the counter of his drugstore on the square. He is a beloved figure. "Pharmacist by trade, mayor by God," a constituent says.

It was the mayor who got the federal money for an interracial commu-nity-center complex that is one of the two or three finest in Mississippi, and they named the tennis courts after him. These tennis courts are used by many people, little black boys playing on a court next to Ole Miss coaches' wives and Dean Faulkner Wells. When a referendum for an integrated swimming pool was turned down, he went to Washington and obtained the funds without a matching clause. He supports the expansion of a large, integrated public housing project. "I swapped the old city hall, so the feds could build a new post office there, for the old federal build-ing, which we made the new city hall. Then we got $359,000 in federal money to remodel the old federal building. Then I got a third of the land I'd swapped for the post office so I could widen the road. That's good manipulatin'.

"Say, we got to live up to Bill Faulkner's spirit in this town," he says. "We got to understand these black kids and help 'em. This is the best damned state in the Union, don't you know it? I don't give a damn if they don't understand us in the North. They don't know what's happen' down here anyway. We're tryin' to live together, black and white. What the hell do they know about *that?*"

In the tradition, and because he is accessible, the citizens play tricks on the mayor. Many of these are telephone calls. "You can't help it," one of the pranksters says. "It's the way he answers the phone—so innocent and friendly and wantin' to help." The finest hoax of all was the unidentified man calling moments before the mayor was closing his drugstore for the night. "My wife needs one of those breast-pump machines. You got one? Can you keep the store open a few minutes longer? She'll be right down." Soon a handsome blond came in and began browsing among the counters. The mayor waited discreetly, then walked over to her. "Do you need a breast pump?" he inquired. She looked straight at him, then furiously departed. Subsequent telephone calls informed the mayor that the ladies of the town were considering a boycott of his store.

"Sure, it was a setup," the mayor said. "She deserved a breast pump. But, hell, they couldn't do without this store. This is where we make public policy—good policy, too, I hope, for Mississippi."

Under the chancellorship of Porter Fortune, a man of integrity, Ole Miss is a different place from its old xenophobic, segregationist image.

A graduate came back not too long ago after an absence of fifteen years. "I can't believe it!" he exclaimed. "It can't be true!" Black and white students together in large numbers. Restaurants that serve wines and spirits. Authentic bars. "X-rated movies in *Oxford, Mississippi!*" He was a product of that era when the students had to drive thirty miles across the Tallahatchie River or forty miles into the delta to buy beer, when one of the flourishing callings was selling bootleg whiskey under the stairwells of the men's dorms, when the coeds had an 11 o'clock curfew, when a restaurant on the square that specialized in New Orleans cuisine would have been unheard of, and when the notion of ten young black men together on a basketball court at one time representing Ole Miss and Mississippi State would have been synonymous with revolution.

The alteration in public drinking habits is especially noteworthy." As long as the people of Mississippi can stagger to the polls," so went the saying of my boyhood in this hard-drinking society, "they'll vote dry." Prohibition was in the state constitution, but the legislature defied all legal reason by collecting a 10 percent black-market tax. The prohibition was repealed in 1966, but there are still immense terrains of dry territory, especially in the parched and fundamentalist hills that are yet serviced by the old-style bootleggers, and even the most casual traveler of the Mississippi byways can discern the moment he leaves a dry county for a wet one by the abrupt appearance at the county line of beer parlors or liquor stores with their numerous blinking lights. On a trip to Yazoo, I was intrigued to discover a new bar on Main Street with a happy hour right out of Madison Avenue. This establishment had been open only a few days. A companion from New York ordered a double martini, and the waitress brought him two martinis.

Much of the ignoble anti-intellectualism of the university has also vanished, certainly of the proselytizing kind. The mean-spiritedness inspired by racism is gone. And from my own experience, the best students are as good as the best students anywhere.

Recently I was talking with one of them who had just returned from visiting a Mississippi friend at Harvard. They had gone to a party and the young man from Ole Miss got into a conversation with a Harvard man.

"Where are you from?" the Mississippian asked.

"What do you mean?"

"Well, where are you from? Where did you go to high school?"

The other young man mentioned an eastern prep school.

"But where did you grow up? Where are your parents?"

"Well, my father is in Switzerland, I think, and my mother is asleep in the next room."

The Ole Miss student told me: "For the first time in my life, I understood that not all Americans are *from* somewhere."

One thing that has not changed at Ole Miss, and likely never will, is the beauty of the sorority girls for which Mississippi is renowned. I call them the Goldfish. The experience of gazing for long moments at goldfish in a bowl is mesmerizing. They adore being looked at, and one senses atavistically that they know you are looking at them as they pause momentarily in their bowl. Yet, except for these instants of reflected narcissism, goldfish rarely remain still for very long, darting about swiftly from one to another, rather mindless in their aquarian pursuits. When the observer places his hand in the bowl, they swim together for cover, wriggling their tail fins.

Ah, the Goldfish! One sees them everywhere in their expensive, brightly colored jogging suits, or coiffured and made up for class. At the Warehouse, you ask one of them what she is majoring in. She looks you exuberantly in the eye and answers: "Fashion merchandising!" Their best boyfriends are usually named Craig or Wallace, who often are not with them but even in their absence are "neat guys," they say, with a "good personality." Sometimes, from the lexicon of the 1950s, they are "sharp" and, on occasion, "real serious about things." The Goldfish are creamy complexioned and keep their toenails painted. On Sorority Row, three months after the election, their Reagan bumper stickers are still on their baby-blue Buicks. God bless the Goldfish! The Ole Miss landscape would be sullen without them, and the outlander must forever be warned: they are smarter and more tenacious than their sunny countenances suggest. For generations the best of these lustrous cyprinids with double names have grown up to run the Sovereign State of Mississippi, just as their great-grandmothers ran the Old Confederacy, their men dying without shoes in the snows of northern Virginia.

Racism has everlastingly been Mississippi's albatross, of course, and in coming home the native son could no more dwell upon his state without its racial background than he could change the color of his eyes. In these years we are seeing a Mississippi that is catching up to the social ideals and values of the older America—the one before Watts or Boston or Detroit, the one of the era when the eastern liberals considered themselves the black southerners' best friends before the black southerners arrived in such numbers, to find that their allies had moved away to Westchester County.

Nowhere has all this been more evident than in the massive integration of the Mississippi public schools, an event that took place only ten years ago. This has brought dislocations, considerable local controversy over aptitude tests and class groupings and a drift to private academies in many of the populous black counties. Yet who a generation ago would have dared predict the day-to-day manifestations of this profound change? It is still so very early, but the emerging biracialism of Mississippi can be seen everywhere—in the newspapers, television, parent-teacher meetings, sports events; in the friendships white and black young-sters have developed in the schools; in a politeness between the races in public places.

The state as a whole is 35 percent black, highest in the nation. Many of the delta counties are well into the 60s, 70s and 80s. Lafayette County—of which Oxford is the county seat—is 26 percent black and 42 percent black in its public schools. In areas of the state with black populations of no more than 35 or 40 percent, the integration of the schools has succeeded beyond anyone's imaginings.

At Ole Miss there are about 700 black students among 10,000. The fraternities and sororities are white, with a handful of black Greek organi-zations. There is a minimum of "social" mingling. In two semesters of teaching literature I have had only one black student. A neighboring professor on the faculty who has been here a long time says that the Ole Miss sorority girl today, with notable exceptions—the ones who care for education and civilization—is little different from her counterpart twenty years ago, with the qualification that "being polite to blacks is part of her repertoire now, just as she had always been polite to the rednecks."

Outside of the public schools, which have not had a single reported racial incident, the two focuses of integration in the community are the athletic department at Ole Miss and, of all places, the bar of the Holiday Inn. Its presiding genius is Clyde Goolsby, a black man of forty who is one of the most popular figures in town and one of the most powerful. "I don't quite know how to say this," a white merchant tells me, "be-cause I'm an old country boy and I grew up the way it was down here, but Clyde's my best friend in the whole world. Damn, I love Clyde! So does everybody else, coloreds and whites. What would this town be with-out him? If we didn't like the ol' mayor so much, we'd run Clyde. Hell, still may."

"Lord, in '62 it took twenty-thousand federal troops to get one black man into Ole Miss," Ed Perry, the state representative, says. "It's New Year's Eve, and here we are sittin' in this bar, white men and women, black men and women, everybody minglin' and usin' first names, all laughin' and jokin' and havin' a good time, and goin' up to Clyde with our troubles, or to get advised about the bowl games, as if everything that moment in '62 represented never even existed. What the hell *happened?*"

"Hey, Tommy!" Clyde shouts at a white patron. "Get off that beer belly and pay me that ten dollars I loaned you."

"Hey, Clyde!" another white client from out in the county yells, "this here's my boy Clarence, goin' to junior college in Senatobia. Clarence, this here's my buddy Clyde."

"Pleased to meet you," Clarence says. "I heard all about you."

"Hope you're better than your pop," Clyde replies, shaking hands.

Later Clyde announces: "I'm switchin' the TV to the ball game *right now.*"

"Aw, come on, Clyde," says one of several white lawyers who are watching a fight. "I got money on round six."

Clyde switches channels. Two black students and a white policeman are playing liar's poker. "Put on that movie *The Great Escape*, Clyde."

"We're watchin' the Hawks and the Knicks," Clyde says, then resumes his conversation with an Ole Miss professor on their theory of human history. The jukebox vies with the basketball game:

> *The bridge washed out,*
> *I can't swim,*
> *And my baby's on the other side. . . .*

Ten years ago I wrote a book about the integration of the public schools in Mississippi; I was in Yazoo on the first day. On perusing that book now, I believe I was right in my premise that in the long sweep of history that event would prove momentous here. I was wrong on certain things too. I misjudged the efficacy and durability of the white private academies in some areas. I misjudged, likewise, the corrosive effects of bedrock poverty on the efforts toward enlightened progress, such as today in the town of Marks, only forty miles west of Oxford in the delta. Martin Luther King, in one of his last public appearances, wept over the condition of its black people. Black unemployment has grown apace with the rise of mechanized farming, and racial bitterness still smolders beneath the more serene surfaces of the 1980s.

Although the access to public institutions has been democratized immeasurably in such a short time, only the future will answer the deeper questions of the Mississippi experiment. Yet it is the little things that accumulate, the constant ironies and juxtapositions that wring the soul and tell much:

—The first black male Ole Miss cheerleader at the Mississippi State football game, lifting a white female cheerleader onto his shoulders before 60,000 spectators.

—The basketball team of the University of Alabama, where George Wallace said he would personally block the main entrance to prevent integration, appearing in the Ole Miss coliseum with one white on its traveling squad.

—At a lunch given by the Ole Miss chancellor, the president of the black students, who is also a Rebel tight end, leaning across the table to tell the wife of a new member of the board of trustees: "What I like about you is your quality of enthusiasm."

Earlier I tried to describe the acutely physical sensations of my returning in the past to all those disparate places I have lived. When I come back now to Oxford, Mississippi, my homecoming seems somehow to bring together the shattered fragments of all those old comings and goings.

Driving up Highway 7 past the little lost hardscrabble towns and the rough exteriors of an isolated America that has been forgotten, I sight the water towers of Ole Miss and the town silhouetted on the horizon, and then the lights of the square and Mr. Bill's courthouse, and the loops and groves of the campus with the Lyceum at the top of the hill, and the dark stadium in the distance. All of it seems to have sprung from the hard red earth for me, as the dispirited Roman legionnaire must have felt on reentering his outpost, his nexus of civilization, after foraging the forlorn stretches of Gaul.

"The writer's vocation," Flaubert wrote, "is perhaps comparable to love of one's native land." If it is true that a writer's world is shaped by the experience of childhood and adolescence, then returning at long last to the scenes of those experiences, remembering them anew and living among their changing heartbeats, gives him, as my writer friend Marshall Frady said, the primary pulses and shocks he cannot afford to lose. I have never denied the poverty, the smugness, the cruelty that have existed in my native state. Meanness is everywhere, but here the meanness, and the nobility, have for me their own dramatic edge, for the fools are *my* fools, and the heroes are mine too.

Yet, finally, when a writer knows home in his heart, his heart must remain subtly apart from it. He must always be a stranger to the place he loves, and its people. His claim to his home is deep, but there are too many ghosts. He must absorb without being absorbed. When he understands, as few others do, something of his home in America—Mississippi—that is funny, or sad, or tragic, or cruel, or beautiful, or true, he knows he must do so as a stranger.

A Love That Transcends Sadness

Not too long ago, in a small Southern town where I live, I was invited by friends to go with them and their children to the cemetery to help choose their burial plot. My friends are in the heartiest prime of life and do not anticipate departing the Lord's earth immediately, and hence, far from being funereal, our search had an adventurous mood to it, like picking out a Christmas tree. It was that hour before twilight, and the marvelous old graveyard with its cedars and magnolias and flowering glades sang with the Mississippi springtime. The honeysuckled air was an affirmation of the tugs and tremors of living. My companions had spent all their lives in the town, and the names on even the oldest stones were as familiar to them as the people they saw every day. "Location," the man of the family said, laughing, "As the real-estate magnates say, we want *location*."

At last they found a plot in the most venerable section which was to their liking, having spurned a shady spot which I had recommended under a giant oak. I knew the caretaker would soon have to come to this place of their choice with a long, thin steel rod, shoving it into the ground every few inches to see if it struck forgotten coffins. If not, this plot was theirs. Our quest had been a tentative success, and we retired elsewhere to celebrate.

Their humor coincided with mine, for I am no stranger to graveyards. With rare exceptions, ever since my childhood, they have suffused me not with foreboding but with a sense of belonging and, as I grow older, with a curious, ineffable tenderness. My dog Pete and I go out into the cemeteries not only to escape the telephone, and those living beings who place more demands on us than the dead ever would, but to feel a continuity with the flow of the generations. "Living," William Faulkner wrote, "is a process of getting ready to be dead for a long time."

I have never been lonely in a cemetery. They are perfect places to

observe the slow changing of the seasons, and to absorb human history—
the tragedies and anguishes, the violences and treacheries, and always the
guilts and sorrows of vanished people. In a preternatural quiet, one can
almost hear the palpable, long-ago voices.

I like especially the small-town cemeteries of America where the children come for picnics and games, as we did when I was growing up—
wandering among the stones on our own, with no adults about, to regard
the mystery and inevitability of death, on its terms and ours. I remember
we would watch the funerals from afar in a hushed awe, and I believe that
was when I became obsessed not with death itself but with the singular
community of death and life together—and life's secrets, life's fears, life's
surprises. Later, in high school, as I waited on a hill to play the echo to
Taps on my trumpet for the Korean War dead, the tableau below with its
shining black hearse and the coffin enshrouded with the flag and the
gathering mourners was like a folk drama, with the earth as its stage.

The great urban cemeteries of New York City always filled me with
horror, the mile after mile of crowded tombstones which no one ever
seemed to visit, as if one could *find* anyone in there even if he wished to.
Likewise, the suburban cemeteries of this generation with their carefully
manicured lawns and bronze plaques embedded in the ground, all imbued
with affluence and artifice, are much too remote for me. My favorites
have always been in the old, established places where people honor the
long dead and the new graves are in proximity with the most ancient.
The churchyard cemeteries of England haunted me with the eternal
rhythms of time. In one of these, years ago as a student at Oxford, I
found this inscription:

> *Here lies Johnny Kongapod,*
> *Have mercy on him, gracious God,*
> *As he would on You if he was God,*
> *And You were Johnny Kongapod*

Equally magnetic were the graveyards of eastern Long Island, with
their patina of the past touched ever so mellowly with the present. The
cemetery of Wainscot, Long Island, only a few hundred yards from the
Atlantic Ocean, surrounded the schoolhouse. I would watch the children
playing at recess among the graves. Later I discovered a man and his

wife juxtaposed under identical stones. On the wife's tomb was "Rest in Peace." On the man's, at the same level, was "No Comment." I admired the audacity of that.

But it is the graveyards of Mississippi which are the most moving for me, having to do, I believe, with my belonging here. They spring from the earth itself, and beckon me time and again. The crumbling stones of my people evoke in me the terrible enigmas of living. In a small Civil War cemetery which I came across recently, the markers stretching away in a misty haze, it occurred to me that most of these boys had never even had a girlfriend. I have found a remote graveyard in the hills with photographs on many of the stones, some nearly one hundred years old, the women in bonnets and Sunday dresses, the men in overalls—"the short and simple annals of the poor." I am drawn here to the tiny grave of a little girl. Her name was Fairy Jumper, and she lived from April 14, 1914, to January 16, 1919. There is a miniature lamb at the top of the stone, and the words: "A fairer bud of promise never bloomed." There are no other Jumpers around her, and there she is, my Fairy, in a far corner of that country burial ground, so forlorn and alone that it is difficult to bear. It was in this cemetery on a bleak February noon that I caught sight of four men digging a grave in the hard, unyielding soil. After a time they gave up. After they left, a man drove toward me in a battered truck. He wanted to know if some fellows had been working on the grave. Yes, I said, but they went away. "Well, I can't finish all by myself." Wordlessly, I helped him dig.

One lonesome, windswept afternoon my dog and I were sitting at the crest of a hill in the town cemetery. Down below us, the acres of empty land were covered with wildflowers. A new road was going in down there, the caretaker had told me; the area was large enough to accommodate the next three generations. "With the economy so bad," I had asked him, "how can you be *expanding?*" He had replied: "It comes in spurts. Not a one last week. Five put down the week before. It's a pretty steady business."

Sitting there now in the dappled sunshine, a middle-aged man and his middle-aged dog, gazing across at the untenanted terrain awaiting its dead, I thought of how each generation lives with its own exclusive solicitudes—the passions, the defeats, the victories, the sacrifices. The names and dates and the faces belong to each generation in its own passing, for much of everything except the most unforgettable is soon forgotten. And yet: though much is taken, much abides. I thought then of human beings, on this cinder of a planet out at the edge of the universe, not knowing where we came from, why we are here, or where we might go after death—and yet we still laugh, and cry, and feel, and love.

"All that we can know about those we have loved and lost," Thornton Wilder wrote, "is that they would wish us to remember them with a more intensified realization of their reality. What is essential does not die but clarifies. The highest tribute to the dead is not grief but gratitude."

At Ole Miss

ECHOES OF A CIVIL WAR'S LAST BATTLE

Twenty years ago this week, the campus of the University of Mississippi was shattered by riots protesting the admission of the first black student. TIME asked Mississippian Willie Morris, the author (North Toward Home, Terrains of the Heart) *and former editor of* Harper's *magazine, to examine changes at Ole Miss since then.*

As one strolls across this hauntingly lovely campus in the beginnings of the great Southern autumn, it is difficult to conceive the chaos and mayhem of Sept. 30, 1962—the gunshots and burning vehicles, the bricks and tear-gas canisters, the federal marshals and National Guardsmen and airborne troops confronting the mob. Two people died, and scores were injured. It was the last battle of the Civil War, the last direct constitutional crisis between national and state authority. James Meredith, a black Air Force veteran, was enrolled as an Ole Miss student the next day. As a native Mississippian, I think of the lines of Yeats:

> *The blood-dimmed tide is loosed, and everywhere*
> *The ceremony of innocence is drowned;*
> *The best lack all conviction, while the worst*
> *Are full of passionate intensity.*

One of the sadnesses was that many Mississippians believed the assurances of their leaders that defiance could succeed. A close friend of impeccable Mississippi lineage (his great-grandfather was wounded in the charge at Gettysburg) was captain of a National Guard unit that was federalized. The other day we were standing on the back porch of my bungalow on the fringes of the campus. He gazed out toward a beautiful wooded terrain. "This was where we dug in," he said. "This was the left flank of our perimeter. We went all the way up to the law school." What impressed him the most, he said, was that the country boys under his command were against everything Meredith was trying to do, yet they were completely loyal to the American flag. He said, tenderly almost, "I guess it must've been the discipline they'd learned in the military."

This is the twentieth anniversary not only of Meredith, but of the death of William Faulkner. He died less than three months before the crisis; he lies now under a towering oak in the town cemetery up the way. The events of that September would likely have broken his heart, as they did the hearts of many Mississippians. "The white people have already lost their heads," he said of those years. "It depends on whether the Negroes can keep theirs." Between then and now there was to be more suffering.

There will be an anniversary observance at Ole Miss this week, and this suggests much about the transfigurations here. The *Ole Miss* magazine, sponsored by the student newspaper, is devoting a special issue to the lessons of that catastrophe. There will be a ceremony under the auspices of the university not far from the Lyceum Building, where one may still see the bullet holes in the façades. It has been organized by Lucius Williams, a black vice chancellor. Awards will be presented to distinguished black graduates. Porter Fortune, the chancellor, a Chapel Hill man who since he came here in 1968 has worked toward making all students feel a part of Ole Miss, will give the welcome. Governor William Winter, a graduate of Ole Miss and one of our most splendid hopes, will attend, and so will Robert Harrison, a black from my home town, Yazoo City, who has just become president of Mississippi's board of trustees for institutions of higher learning. The keynote speaker will be Margaret Walker Alexander, the black novelist and teacher. Meredith, now a businessman in Jackson, has been invited to speak.

The ironies of Mississippi have forever baffled the outsider, as they should. Two and a half years after Meredith's admission, Governor Ross Barnett's principal antagonist of that time, Bobby Kennedy, gave the commencement address at Ole Miss. He was introduced by Senator Jim Eastland and received a standing ovation. Twelve years after the event, Ben Williams, also of Yazoo City, the first black football player at Ole Miss, was elected Colonel Rebel by the student body, the highest honor for a male student. (He is now with the Buffalo Bills.) More recently, Mississippi's Leontyne Price was named honorary alumna, and for weeks an exhibit depicting her life was displayed in the library. John Slaughter, the black physicist, was the commencement speaker last spring.

In the broader context, Mississippi's black population of 37 percent is the highest for any state. Mississippi is also, of course, the poorest state; its poverty exacerbates every issue. Alone in America, it has no state-supported system of kindergartens, and earlier this year the legislature defeated Governor Winter's kindergarten bill, which would mainly have benefited poor black children. Conversely, the congressional race this fall in the Second District, which mostly comprises the Delta, strikes into the very core of everything Mississippi and the South could become. A black man, Robert Clark, an influential legislator, won the Democratic nomination this summer with substantial white support and faces a Reagan Republican in November. He could become the first black Congressman from Mississippi since Reconstruction. The integration of the public schools, which took place in 1970, is working beyond one's most sanguine hopes in those areas where the black population is less than 50 percent; it is a different story in the counties of the Delta. Mississippi today is a blend of the relentless and the abiding.

There are about 700 black students at Ole Miss out of an enrollment of 10,000, or 7 percent. The university actively recruits blacks and encourages their participation in extracurricular activities. The Ole Miss football team is roughly half black; the basketball team predominantly black. In a society where organized sports are more than a ritual, Ole Miss partisans cheer their black players as enthusiastically as they do the whites, and the outstanding ones are authentic campus heroes.

Like the university, Oxford has a population of 10,000. It is the fifth smallest town in the U.S. to serve as the seat of a capstone state university. There are only seven full-time undergraduate black professors; Meredith himself says he is reluctant now to praise an institution with so few black teachers and students. Money is one problem, and black professors and administrators are often lost to larger schools. The rural backdrop is another, as is the absence of a sizable middle-class black community. The Black Student Union and the Associated Student Body have recently merged. But the pervasive sorority and fraternity systems remain segregated; the blacks have their own chapters.

Many blacks complain that they do not feel they are a significant part of campus life. I was privy to this emotion in a small class I taught last semester. I had encouraged the young whites and blacks to be candid about the realities of their relationships here. What ensued was sudden and torrential. The blacks said they found it difficult to consider this their university. The whites said they were trying to understand. One white youngster was especially disarming. "I have nothing against you," he said of the blacks. "In fact, I like you. I think if there were more of you, the situation would be better."

I have heard other stories. In a zoology class of thirty-six students, mostly white sorority girls, no one chose to be the laboratory partner of the only black male student. After an embarrassing interval, a white girl who was not in a sorority volunteered. In a class that was discussing the Meredith riots, a black student argued: "Only the vocabulary has changed. How many black professors are there? How many administrators?" A white private-school graduate replied, "If things are so bad, why are you here?" During this discussion, two white sorority girls were thumbing through *Vogue* magazine.

It is a sensitive dialogue suffused with consequence. One young white says, "It's like they separate themselves from us." A graduate student argues, "The blacks on campus permit tokenism, and the whites promote it." A black teacher observes, "For many whites and blacks, rapport is not a natural thing. People have to learn it." And so the litany goes.

A final contention lies in the traditional symbols of the Old South. Many blacks complain of the school fight song *Dixie*, the mascot Colonel Rebel, and the waving of the Confederate battle flag at athletic events. The university's first black cheerleader, John Hawkins of Water Valley, Mississippi, attracted attention before the first football game of this season when he announced he would not carry the Confederate flag on the field. His wishes were understood by both the administration and many of the students. Hawkins, as well as Steven Sloan, the fine young Ole Miss football coach, favors a modified Rebel flag with "Ole Miss" or "U.M." superimposed on the venerable Stars and Bars. This proposal is gaining wide favor. As for *Dixie*, the Ole Miss band, which has many black performers, has perfected a number, called *From Dixie with Love,* that is a stirring blend of *Dixie* and *The Battle Hymn of the Republic.* Their rendition would touch the soul of a Massachusetts abolitionist.

It is the accumulation of such ironies, so meaningful to the native son, that makes this beautiful and tragic and bewitched state unique. It is no accident that Mississippi elicits such rage and passion and fidelity in its sons and daughters of both races, or that Northerners have always been obsessed with what takes place here, for Mississippi has always been the crucible of the national guilt. Much remains to be accomplished, although there is a tolerance of independent expression in Mississippi now that does its own deepest traditions proud. With the flourishing of that tolerance, the young whites and blacks of Ole Miss have more in common than they may for the moment think. They spring mutually from a traditional order and, more than any other young Americans, they know how to make a story and spin a tale. Public high school graduating classes last spring were the first in which whites and blacks attended all twelve grades together. After all of its pain, and the difficulty to come, this could be, in truth, the only society in America where "the great plan," as the rest of the nation has intermittently conceived of it, could some day succeed.

Allison Brown, daughter of an old white Mississippi family, honor student, campus beauty, and editor of the Meredith issue of the *Ole Miss* magazine, has written for her editorial: "We are of a generation in Mississippi who knows firsthand that blacks and whites can actually work together, grow up together, and share common experiences. Even at Ole Miss, where tradition hangs on until the very last thread, much progress has been made. . . . Our generation can do something about it. We can work toward the inevitable changes that will make Ole Miss a better place for people of all races."

Now That I Am Fifty

Everyone with luck and the penchant for life turns fifty. "It's no big deal," a friend said to me just today. When I turned twenty-one, in a dubious nocturnal roadhouse near Austin, Texas, someone inexplicably smashed a beer bottle over my head. And when I regained consciousness, the lines of A. E. Housman, which a University of Texas professor had ceremoniously read to me that day, rang through my dizzied brain:

> *When I was one-and-twenty*
> *I heard a wise man say.*
> *"Give crowns and pounds and guineas*
> *But not your heart away;*
> *Give pearls away and rubies*
> *But keep your fancy free."*
> *But I was one-and-twenty,*
> *No use to talk to me.*

A few years later, as I was on a college lecture tour during the turbulent Vietnam time, a student at a Midwestern school taunted me. "I don't trust anyone over thirty," he said. "What do you think of that?" I replied that I did not trust anyone *under* thirty—they lacked experience, were self-righteous, and ignorant of the rhythms of history. Further, I trusted no one *over* thirty, obsessed as they were with material things, too eager to compromise. "How old are *you?*" the young man wanted to know. "I'm thirty," I said.

Forty vanished like a pebble in a pond, a most overrated juncture, more important to women, perhaps, than to men. And now comes fifty, and what does one make of *that*, and how does one fit *this* into the deep and cosmic order?

I have existed in my lifetime across the spectrum of society, dined with the leaders and frequented the back of the barrooms, known the people who run the world and the ones who drive the pickup trucks. I have been profoundly in love, and profoundly out of it. I have dwelled in the metropolitan places and in the urban ones, sojourned in Paris, France, and in Paris, Texas, in Oxford, England, and in Oxford, Mississippi, and I am surely the only man from Yazoo to have visited Wahoo.

I am haunted by my own guilts and self-pities, by the cruel and foolish things I have done. Many is the day I have felt myself part of the kingdom of the monkeys. I have suffered quintessentially the old Anglican injunction: Is it worse to have done what one ought not to have done or to have left undone what one ought to have done? I have whispered the pledge from Mark Harris's *Bang the Drum Slowly:* "From here on in I rag nobody." I have sensed life so imperceptibly slipping away, yet I still know the childlike experience of waking up and wanting to explore the day. The time to hang up the spikes, the old baseball men said, is when you get tired of putting on the uniform. Perhaps fifty is younger than thirty, when a man really feels old. Yet underneath it all are the secret fears most people share: fear of failure, fear of success, fear of hurt and love.

After fifty years, what is truly important in one's life? What really matters? Whom does one trust? Whom does one love?

Time and remembrance matter. Memory is a release from the narrowness of circumstance; it gives one a sense that there is something beyond the miserable details of everyday life. Fragments of memory may seem like shards of broken glass—the summer sounds of childhood, the whistle of a train taking you far away, the tender look of someone you loved— but to me there is a fragile touch of immortality in them. They give us a breath of continuity.

The ghosts are all around me, of those I loved now across the divide; I have learned the silence of the grave. Is death, too, merely part of the adventure? I have a recurring dream, a strange reverie, of entering a favorite place I once knew, a dimly lit restaurant on the great Eastern littoral with Tiffany lamps and a mahogany bar. As I come in, the dozens of people there turn and see me. They are all people I have cared for who are dead, not a living person among them, and they greet me one by one with warmth and affection, as in Fellini's dance of mortality.

I have an eight-year-old friend named Cap who phoned on the death of my aged Black Labrador to see how I was doing. He offered to save his money and buy me another one. "Little puppies," he remarked, "last longer than old dogs."

My young comrade will discover soon enough that, in the nature of things and at least by my count, about one in every seven or eight humans is cruel, mean-spirited, or destructive, that they also are part of life and that he will encounter them at Manhattan cocktail parties as surely as he will in the bleakest boondocks and most sordid canebrakes, not to mention in utopian settlements, the councils of emerging nations, poets' conventions, and church communions. I hope he will learn, too, that thought and reasoning are nothing if they do not buttress and nourish the human processes and that those individuals of intelligence, kindness, imagination, courage, sensibility, and fun who grace his life will be worth the courting.

"Tho' much is taken, much abides," wrote Tennyson in the poem "Ulysses." As I age, it is not the grandiose equations that abide, but family, friendship, community. It is important for me to feel at one with a beloved place, its cadences and continuities. Or to feel about family, as I recently overheard a friend say to his son, "I couldn't make it without you."

We cannot choose our families, but we can our friends. One recalls from uncomprehending adolescence the poem of Emily Brontë:

> *Love is like the wild rose-briar,*
> *Friendship like the holly-tree—*
> *The holly is dark when the rose-briar blooms*
> *But which will bloom most constantly?*

No matter what one feels or dreams or fears in one's loneliest being, others among us have felt or dreamed or feared these things too. There is a community of the heart, and friendship is the closest community of all.

Mitch and the Infield Fly Rule

When I first came down to Ole Miss a few years back to be "writer-in-residence," I taught a course on the modern American novel. The English Department picked out for me, they reported, seventy-five of the best students at the university. We met twice a week in a sizeable lecture hall built like an amphitheater.

The reading list, I shall say, was substantial but somewhat eclectic. I had designed it to bring down a few authors. William Styron, John Knowles, and Gloria Jones (James Jones's widow) came free of charge to discuss *Sophie's Choice, A Separate Peace,* and *From Here to Eternity,* and so did George Plimpton, Jack Whitaker, and Michael Burke to talk about their friendships with novelists.

It was heady fare. One afternoon, in the middle of my lecture on *Go Down, Moses,* from the back of the hall I heard an ungodly noise—a kind of exaggerated yawn, a plaintive cry of ennui and exasperation. My God, I thought, I'm boring them to death. It turned out, however, to be my black Labrador Pete, who had come into the room before I had arrived and was sleeping on the floor of the back row.

Ole Miss has forever been noted for its beautiful coeds. It has had several Miss Americas, and I will confess there were quite a few lovely girls in that class. They served to encourage the Socratic method. On fine spring days they would arrive en masse in shorts and halters and sit on the front rows, unmercifully tormenting their middle-aging teacher; sometimes my dog Pete came in with them. The most beautiful of all was a willowy, full-breasted blond Chi Omega, twenty-one years old, tall and slender and lithesome with a throaty Bacall voice, wry and irreverent and whimsical, a fount of good cheer. And a straight-A student! We called her "Mitch." I had given her a 96 on her report on Walker Percy's *The Moviegoer.* She told me she identified with the troubled male protagonist, Binx Bolling of New Orleans. I should not even have to write this: I was secretly in love with her, of course.

I had Mark Harris's novel of baseball and death, <u>*Bang the Drum*</u> <u>*Slowly*</u>, on the reading list. I tried unsuccessfully to get Mark Harris himself to journey down, and then on impulse I asked Jake Gibbs, the Ole Miss baseball coach who had spent ten years as a catcher with the Yankees, to lecture on the book.

"You say it's about a catcher?" Jake asked as he spit a little Levi Garrett under the bleachers during practice.

I told him yes, and even added that he would not have to deal with symbolism or divine any existentialist meaning. But Jake had a home doubleheader on the appointed day against Boo Ferriss's Delta State University club and declined the invitation, with considerable relief, I sensed.

On the night before the class, I was sitting at the bar of the Warehouse off the courthouse square and sighted Mitch at a table with friends. I asked her to join me for a minute.

"What is it, Prof?" she asked.

"How would you like to earn a bottle of ice-cold Moët & Chandon?" I said.

She glanced at me apprehensively. "What do I have to do?"

"You've got a good memory. Just memorize this word for word and quote it when I call on you tomorrow." I furtively withdrew from my coat *The Sporting News'* pocket-sized *Official Baseball Rules* and pointed to a section on page eighteen.

"What is it?" she said, looking down.

"The infield fly rule."

"The *what?*"

No need for questions, I said. "Just memorize it. And remember that the reason for the rule is that an infielder in this situation could drop the ball on purpose and then turn an easy double play." She asked me to repeat this rationale, then promised to be ready.

It was a pristine afternoon for baseball. The windows of the lecture hall were open to let in the honeyed scents of Deep Southern April. The baseball field was across the street, and we could hear the sounds of bat-on-ball and the roar of the crowd in the soft, languid sunshine.

I gave my lecture on *Bang the Drum Slowly*, then asked questions. Mr. Bill Rhodes of Indianola had just addressed himself well to a singular irony: the catcher got better and better the closer he came to death. Yet death itself seemed a chimera on this matchless day of spring.

Five minutes remained in the class when I posed the last question.

"Who can identify the infield fly rule?" I asked.

"The *what?*" one of the coeds said.

"Infield fly rule."

There was an awkward, deepening silence among the Ole Miss scholars. Then a big old boy from the Delta raised his hand.

"Mr. Edwards."

"With runners on first and third with two outs, if the batter. . . ."

"Wrong. Anyone else?"

A smart black Ole Miss Rebel basketball player from Memphis now raised his hand: "With runners on second and third and only one out. . . ."

"Wrong again," I said. *"Anyone?"*

They whispered embarrassedly among themselves.

"They tell me you're the best students in all of the University of Mississippi—and not a single one of you can recite the infield fly rule."

After a further pause, from the front row there was another hand. Mitch was wearing blue shorts and a crimson halter. She reminded me in that instant of Candice Bergen in *Carnal Knowledge.*

"Miss Mitchell," I said.

In her deep, lilting Dixie voice she replied, enunciating each word: "An infield fly is a fair fly ball—not including a line drive nor an attempted bunt—which can be caught by an infielder with ordinary effort, when first and second, or first, second, and third bases are occupied, before two are out. The pitcher, catcher, and any outfielder who stations himself in the infield on the play shall be considered infielders for the purpose of this rule."

A cataclysmic rustle filled the big room. Everyone was gazing at her in astonishment. She continued:

"When it seems apparent that a batted ball will be an infield fly, the umpire shall immediately declare 'Infield Fly,' for the benefit of the runners. The ball is alive and runners may advance at the risk of being caught, or retouch and advance after the ball is touched, the same as on any fly ball."

"That's good, Miss Mitchell."

"Wait. I'm not finished."

"Of course. Continue."

"On the infield fly rule the umpire is to rule whether the ball could *ordinarily* have been handled by an infielder—not by some arbitrary limitation such as the grass, or the base lines. The infield fly is in no sense to be considered an appeal play. The umpire's judgment must govern, and the decision should be made immediately."

From the back of the hall students were standing up to get a better view of her as she recited. "I can't believe this," one young man exclaimed.

"What is the reason for this rule?" I asked.

"Perfectly simple," she replied. "An infielder in this situation could drop the ball on purpose and then turn an easy double play. I always thought this a fine rule."

At that very moment the bell sounded. As Mitch left, the crowd parted to let her through. I believe they wanted to touch the hem of her garment—the crimson halter.

I caught up with her alone just beyond Bondurant Hall. "How about a bottle of Moët & Chandon at the Warehouse, Mitch?"

"How about two?" she said.

Here Lies My Heart

It is a shrill and misty Manhattan dusk: autumn 1969. A wan sliver of dying sunlight catches the windows of the skyscrapers. I am standing furtively at a street corner. Soon my wife emerges from a door across the way. No—my *ex*-wife. We have been divorced a fortnight, though I have yet to acknowledge the reality. I have been waiting here for her; I know she is the psychiatrist's last client of the afternoon, and that he himself will sooner or later come out, too. I watch as she drifts away into the New York manswarm, receding from me like a pebble in a pond, my college sweetheart. My heart literally palpitates with rage and fear and guilt, all of it so horrendously vainglorious, yet it is the man I have come to see, as if merely knowing what he *looks* like might ease some grievous wrong.

For weeks I have harbored the vengeful incubus that he and he alone has razed my marriage. That even had she been an ax murderess he would have counseled her, as surely they all did in that histrionic and debilitating American era: "Do what you must to be happy. If it feels good, do it." The *presumption* of him: He is my faceless bête noire, incognito as the great city night, and he has unleashed my most ferocious Confederate tantrums. Frequently have I been tempted to compose for him epistles of nearly Herzogian sweep, have even seriously contemplated what I imposed upon cruelhearted adults in my small-town Mississippi childhood: gift-wrapped fresh cow manure or dead rats or possums deposited on their front porches in the yuletide.

The mist has turned now into a grim, unhurried rain. Everywhere is the anguished bedlam of the Manhattan Sixties, the panhandlers, the junkies, the crowds so dense that people appear to be standing in queues just to walk down sidewalks, the staccato clamor of the jackhammers, the steam pouring upward from the sewers as if the world underneath were an inferno, the tall, ominous visage of buildings, so of death, others' and my own. What indeed if someone drops a big mahogany table out a top window and it lands right on me? Such then is my midtown paranoia, real now as my darkest nightmares.

Then, suddenly, he emerges from the same doorway. In stark intuition I know it is he. My heart begins beating fast, and surreptitiously I hasten across the raucous thoroughfare for a closer view. In my anonymous khaki trench coat I could be Gene Hackman tailing the Gallic drug czar down these same streets in *The French Connection*.

I am nearing him now as he pauses at a newsstand in the Gotham ritual of buying the afternoon's *Post,* then *The Village Voice*. I slip into an aperture near a Chock Full O'Nuts and observe him. He is of medium height and wears a gray overcoat. He is young! He looks innocent! He has red hair! This is my final subjugation. I really want him to look like Bernard Malamud. As he walks away I consider moving in on him at the flank, in the manner of Stonewall at Chancellorsville, confronting him nostril to nostril, as Lyndon Johnson did in that way with special antagonists, demanding what arcane knowledge he has appropriated of our joys and sufferings and the things we shared together: the fragrant spring twilights at our university those years ago, the gallant Longhorns whipping the loathsome Aggies, the catfish and beer in the Balcones Hills, the midnight chimes at Oxford, the birth of our child, the old love and promise and hope. Then helplessly I watch as he descends into the steely entrails of the asphalt earth as New Yorkers do, down deep to the rattling IRT, disappearing forever toward whatever cramped Bronx domicile lends him sequester for his cosmic jurisdictions.

All that was more than twenty years ago, another lifetime really, and during my tenure in the East, nearly three marriages in four were ending in divorce. One summer forenoon in the Hamptons, at a lawn party off a blue and sparkling inlet, I gazed across at the celebrants, some fifty couples I more or less knew from the city: With only two or three exceptions, I was drawn in an instant to note, everyone there had been divorced at least once. Among my contemporaries in those days there seemed a profound desperation about abiding relationships. I searched my friends who had dwelled in the crucible of them for answers, but I found that they knew nothing I did not know. So, as with me, since self-righteousness is surely the mightiest mode of survival, the blame fell on the partner. Everyone was too highly keyed, seething with fickle introspection and aggrandizement. Nothing lasted. It all seemed of a piece with the American Sixties.

She and I were very young when we married, and a very long way too from the East. The Almighty has always been southern in that regard: Get on early with the pristine charter of procreation. One of the clichés of the day held that young marriage was singularly desirable; you would "grow up together," the irony being that growing up can also mean growing apart.

Nonetheless, it survived eleven years, across many terrains, American and otherwise, in good times and bad, and the denouement was terrible, and more than one would ever have bargained for, and the trauma of the ultimate break lasted longer than its duration. The anger, bafflement, jealousy, and sting threatened never to go away, and their scar tissue is probably on my heart forever. Yet whose *fault* was it? I ask myself now, hundreds of miles and a whole generation removed. And what did it say about ourselves? And what on earth did it mean? As with many strange and faraway things in one's life, one wonders, did it ever mean anything at all?

She came from a raw and sprawling metropolis on the rise, I from the flatland and canebrakes of deepest Dixie. I remember as yesterday the first time I ever saw her. I was playing in a fraternity intramural football game, and I sighted her on the sidelines talking with some friends, a stunningly beautiful, dark-complexioned brunette, and she was caught for me in a frieze of mirthful laughter, and to this day I could show you the precise spot near the university where we first kissed. The two of us were important on the campus in those languid Eisenhower years. I was editor of the student daily; she was a Phi Beta Kappa and was even elected "Sweetheart of the University"; five thousand students sang "The Eyes of Texas" to her in the school gymnasium. On my twenty-first birthday she gave me a book of English verse, and she wrote in it the inscription:

> *Grow old with me,*
> *The best is yet to be,*
> *The last for which the first is made.*

We were married in a chapel in her city, not far from where she grew up. My father died while we were on our honeymoon, and I remember the passion and the grief.

Not many American marriages begin in that Home of Lost Causes, that City of Dreaming Spires—Oxford. I had a scholarship, and to this day I cannot believe we were actually there. There were the impenetrable fogs, the chimes at midnight in the High, always too many bells ringing in the rain. Arm in arm we strolled through the gardens and hidden places of the magical town, reveling in its bleak gray treasures. A wing of an old house was ours, surrounded by lush gardens, the Isis twisting upon itself in the emerald distance. The bachelor Yanks were eternally there, all of them a little in love with her.

On a cold and frosty Christmas Eve, the two of us sat at the high mass in the cathedral of King's College, Cambridge. There was a thin skein of snow on the magnificent sweeping quadrangle outside, and the wonderful stained glass and the elaborate flickering candlelight and the resounding organ and the grand processional in Henry VIII's vaulted chamber, the little English boys in their red ceremonial robes coming ever so slowly down the aisles with their flags and maces, their voices rising, and this was one of the most beautiful things we would ever see in our lives, and we were happy. And then a term break in Paris, and I am walking up Rue Git-le-Coeur, which abuts the Seine, and with the ineffable sights and sounds I conjure Gershwin, and soon there she is, leaning indolently against the upper balcony of our pension, five months pregnant and in a red dress, looking mischievously down at me as I approach, and her sunny words come down through time: "My distinguished husband."

After that, our heady New York days were suffused with happiness, and then slowly advancing pain. Did the city itself implant the seeds of our own growing recklessness? We were Upper West Side people, back when the Upper West Side was an authentic neighborhood, and at nighttime in the Vietnam years came the echoes of sirens and mayhem from Columbia up the way. On the very day she received her Ph.D. in Bryant Park, Bobby Kennedy was shot.

The fields of fame and ambition grew heavy with pitfalls, though I doubt either of us would have acknowledged that then. Imperceptibly at first, our lives became tense and theatrical—all of celebrity's appurtenances. I was editor of a national magazine, she a young scholar, and our lives converged portentously with the great writers, the critics, the publishers, the millionairesses, the Hollywood heroines, the avatars of the moment's culture: dinner at Clare Booth Luce's or Bennett Cerf's or Punch Sulzberger's, literary celebrations, our photographs in the newsweeklies and newspapers. It happened all too swiftly. In our provincial years our friends thought we would last forever because we were so similar, mainly, I suspect, because we liked books, yet almost against our mutual will we were seeming to become so *different*—had we always been, I wonder, but lacked the experience to see it?—one of us introspective, academic, and disciplined, the other inchoate, nocturnal, uncompromisingly headstrong. How to explain such things, or even to remember them and be honest about them, for memory itself selects and expurgates and diffuses. It was not as fun as it had been.

We bought a farmhouse in the country, even acquired a black Lab puppy to shore up the marriage, and the small-town boy actually joined the anonymous phalanx of Harlem Line commuters in the summer, but the real trouble was just beginning. Doubt is inherent in any reality. She had begun to doubt, and doubt is a contagious hazard, yet the arguments, the insecurities, the melancholies, the insomnias, the inconstancies had to be symptomatic of something deeper, more elusive and mysterious.

All these merged in a daily tangle of hostility and distrust, punctuated by chilly, apprehensive silences. Silence speaks for itself, of course, and there were nights when I did not come home; our precocious love mocked us now, those threads of faded affection seemed frivolous and meaningless, and before our very eyes we had become rivals and antagonists.

The day came when she ordered me from the apartment. Where to go? What to take? I had to escape the city; a confused weekend in Connecticut with friends: "God, you look awful!" The mirror betrayed a complexion sallow as parchment, rings under the eyes like obsidian blisters, and I was developing a wicked little rash about the neck, what we once called *risin's* in Mississippi. Now we were in the deepening maw of divorce, a desolate subterrain all its own. The lawyers, of course, took over—mine a breezy man, cynical and unfeeling, hers hard and profes-

The John Foster Dulles

In the faraway spring of 1957, three of my Yank chums and I, in our first year at Oxford University, were plotting a trip to Rome by way of Paris and Avignon during the long spring break. We concluded we needed a car to get us there. English friends counseled us that the most efficacious bargain, one that could take us around the world twice over and pay for itself multifold, would be a retired London taxicab, the square rectangular kind then in vogue, which would cost fifty quid or so, about $150 then.

For this mission we dispatched Ooms of Amherst and Yoder of Chapel Hill to London. They spent most of a March weekend exploring the surreptitious lots of the ancient gray town. There were no discarded taxis to be found. Their diligent research, however, led them to one Captain Buckley-Johnson of the Bayswater neighborhood, who wished to dispose of a magnificent slate-blue Buick town car, vintage 1927. Ooms and Yoder reported that Captain Buckley-Johnson was enthusiastic to sell it, and at our budget price of fifty quid.

The following week, Baker of Chapel Hill and I went to London to bring our town car back to Oxford. Somewhere in the Chiltern Hills, something began to shake in the motor, an ominous grinding accompanied by enormous spirals of steam and smoke. We chugged into Oxford and allowed the radiator to cool for three or four days.

We named the Buick "John Foster Dulles" after our peregrinating Secretary of State of that era. The afternoon of our odyssey arrived. We had parked "Foster" in the quadrangle of my college, New College, which had been new in 1379, not far from the eleventh-century Old City Wall. As American and German tourists gawked in incredulity, many of them taking photographs of "typical" Oxford students, we christened Foster with a Coca-Cola.

There were five of us in the leather seats of Foster's copious confines—we four proprietors and Suddarth of Yale, who had been reluctant to participate in the ambitious investment but had talked his way into a free ride to Paris. Our aim was to reach Dover for the ferry across the English Channel to Calais. I was at the wheel near the Anglo-Saxon hamlet of Dorchester-on-Thames when there was a sudden, piercing explosion. The left rear tire had expired. I managed to maneuver Foster off the road. We got out and examined the derelict tire. The dark green countryside was empty and bereft. In that instant, as if by divination, a diminutive fellow in immaculate uniform from the Royal Automobile Club appeared on a motorcycle. He wordlessly saluted and without our so much as asking began repairing the tire. When he had finished I led him out of earshot of my companions.

"Will this car get us to Rome?" I asked.

"To *Rome*, sir? I wouldn't count on it, sir. I rather doubt it will make Dover." I did not share this dire assessment with the others.

Baker was the pilot now as we moved through the miniature land in the encroaching darkness. The others were discussing Rome, and what the girls must be like. In a tiny village of Surrey we began looking for a pub. As we turned sharply at an innocent corner there came a sound I had never before or since heard in an automobile, a succession of esoteric bumping scrapes, metronomic in their intensity, soon followed by a strange hissing sensation, and then an horrific sort of blast.

"Now look what's happened," Baker shouted. "The wheel's come off!"

"I knew we'd have problems," the interloper Suddarth said.

"Oh, shut up, Rocky!" Baker turned petulantly to our future ambassador to Jordan. "You don't even own this car."

The wheel had not come off, but another rear tire was hopelessly shredded, like rubber confetti. There was a garage nearby, and we asked the proprietor the price of two additional tires. He was all courtesy, but was not able to suppress a laugh. To his knowledge, tires for a 1927 American Buick, he said, had not been sold in England since some time before World War II.

The five of us spent the night in Foster, which was attached to the end of a towing truck at a forty-five-degree angle. Was it all a loss? We never made it to Rome, but at least we had come within striking distance of the Channel. At some point in that chilled late March night, we drew straws to see whom of us would return to London to salvage a portion of our investment from Captain Buckley-Johnson. This time Yoder, Ooms, and Baker were the emissaries. Buckley-Johnson took Foster back and reimbursed us most of the money. "He reacted as an officer and a gentleman," Yoder later reported. "I've been a fervent believer in the Anglo-Saxon Alliance ever since."

The non-owner Suddarth and I were the winners of the draw and arrived by the boat-train in Paris on a luminous afternoon of April 1, 1957. After the severe English winter, the magic city unfolded for us in all its vibrance and beauty. We began exploring it forthwith, with no guilt whatever that our comrades were still in England negotiating our rebate. Not too long ago, I ran into Suddarth for the first time in thirty-five years, at a state dinner for King Hussein and Queen Noor of Jordan in the East Room of the White House. He had flown into Washington with the King and Queen and their royal retinue and had just finished chatting with George Bush when he spotted me. He approached me swiftly. "Say, Morris," Ambassador Suddarth asked, "whatever do you think came of John Foster Dulles?"

As the Years Go By, Do We Grow Crankier—Or More Tolerant?

A couple of months ago, on my sixty-first birthday, a comrade jocularly asked, "Do you see yourself growing more intolerant, or more tolerant?" It was a beguiling question, and a very human one, touching on many aspects of aging; and because it titillated me I have been thinking about it.

I truthfully believe I have grown more tolerant with time, and I will try to explain some of the reasons why. More than a year ago, almost coincidental with my turning sixty, something exceedingly strange and unexpected began to happen in my life. I had always been an easy and heavy sleeper, but suddenly I began to awaken regularly at the first light of dawn, whereupon my precipitously troubled consciousness would enter into a hazy reverie of years long past, a drowsing yet sleepless musing often lasting as long as three hours or more. During these hours, I would dwell upon, in graphic and painful detail, one by one in aimless progression, specific past guilts of my lifetime: errors, transgressions, cruelties, fears—the back-stabbing of a long-ago professional colleague, or a deceitful act to a friend, or monstrous behavior to a person I cared for, or a dreadfully unthinking remark that hurt someone, and on and on in these old peremptory mists, almost as in a shadowy Fellini film. Not unlike Mr. Scrooge himself, I am visited daily now by these unrelenting spirits evoking my own accumulated neglects and flaws, not at night as happened with Scrooge, but in the *morning*.

One such morning, for instance, I was compelled to the recollection of my standing before the honor society of which I was a member at my university and successfully opposing the nomination of a young man who was about to be my opponent for the editorship of the student newspaper. On another, I was obsessed with the image of striking and knocking down a small African-American child when I was twelve years old. Or of telling my mother in a tantrum of bad temper that I did not love her.

Or of mindlessly publishing off-the-record comments of a public official when I was twenty-five on a statewide paper and getting him into serious trouble. Or of angrily taking the wedding ring from my wife's finger when I was thirty-two and tossing it out the window of a New York apartment. Or of writing something at age forty-eight of an adversary that I knew bordered on libel. Or of making a buffoon of myself at age fifty at the wedding of friends by losing my composure and cursing the future father-in-law. Such venerable self-pities and selfish aggrandizements and awkward indispositions occurred in dozens of venues. The catalog is endless.

I do not know the sources of these horrific visitations and the dark, brooding nightmares that accompany them. I wish I did. But somehow they have begun to mellow me and make me a little more charitable—how could they not? They have helped me realize that I am far from perfect myself: that we are all flawed creatures springing from the ambivalence of our common inheritance and must pray for more indulgence of the fallibilities of our fellows. And with all this, some slight or injury or deception over which I have been aggrieved, from something that happened to me last week, or six months ago, or eight years ago, mysteriously begins to recede into the retrospective tally of my own complex and melancholy remembrances.

Not that I am lost in a delicate cloud of benevolence, but I feel I have become more forgiving of others' transgressions toward *me*. Here are some examples. Recently a man I thought a friend bitterly attacked me, grossly unfairly I thought, as a person and a writer in an interview with a newspaper. In earlier days, I would have responded with ire. Instead, after my initial anger, I tried to reflect on the reasons he had chosen to be so offensive and let it go at that. Later, when a recent book of mine came out, a prominent magazine published what I considered the most abusively hostile review of any in my long lifetime as a writer, taking gratuitous liberties with something that took me three years to write. I have never once written to a book reviewer, but twenty years ago I would surely have answered this one in kind, or even gone so far as to confront the man personally. Now I let this drop also; this is part of the territory, I told myself.

Similarly, my recollections of *past* affronts—someone years ago who attempted to get my job, or a friend who tried to convince my wife to leave me, or a stranger who wrote destructive letters about me to my professional colleagues—are no longer so enveloped in distant distrusts and paranoias, but oddly begin to fit for me into some vast and profoundly unfathomable human puzzle.

Ironically, my spectral post-dawn visions come at the happiest time in my personal life: I have a loving and talented son, more money than I have ever made, a beautiful old house set in verdant Southern terrain, a new marriage more contented than I ever could have hoped for, two inspiriting stepsons and four exasperating yet affectionate cats who are now songs in the heart of this former feline misanthrope. From a long bachelorhood of divorce in the literary enclaves of New York and then in a sequestered college town to this tranquil landing near the place of my birth in Jackson, Mississippi, I am learning to see my existence as a whole, as a funny integrity, as part of the quintessence of life and death.

Much of this is reflected in my own writer's calling. After a lifetime as a writer and editor of such magazines as *The Texas Observer* and *Harper's*, where my job involved tough criticism of those I considered adversaries, what I really wish to do now is write about people and places and things that intrigue me, that I admire.

Not too long ago, a widely read magazine offered me a very lucrative assignment for what would be its cover story on a prominent national figure. I pondered this offer, watched the man on television, listened to him on the radio, took notes, but finally told the editors I would not do the piece because I felt no human chemistry with him, indeed could not abide him nor anything he stood for. At age thirty-five, I would have taken the assignment with much enthusiasm.

There are other factors, too. I believe my returning home to the place of my birth has substantially mellowed me. I do not consider it odd that I often drive the forty miles or so from the city where I live to the small town where I grew up and take long solitary walks, the streets and alleys so etched in my memory—the cemetery, the school, the house where my dog Skip lies buried in the backyard. I amble past the dwellings of the reprobates and charlatans we feared in that boyhood time, all long dead, everything evanescently touched by the patina of the vanished years.

In my first book, *North Toward Home*, I described moving to New

York City and seeing everywhere people whom I thought I knew from my hometown. Now, on returning home after all the years, I see them in reality, running into them in restaurants or supermarkets, resuming conversations that might have been broken in midsentence decades ago. At the Jitney Jungle check-out last week, a vaguely familiar figure accosted me: "Do you know who I am?" In an instant I replied: "Billy Rhodes!" My warm-spirited boyhood pal and I discussed the ball games we played in and the girls we dated, and he brought out photos of his grandchildren.

As I age, and since I dwell in a relatively settled society, I perceive now more than I ever did the link between the generations—the continuity. It is not uncommon in my hometown for three generations of the same families I have known to still live there. I am constantly confusing the generations, talking with a son or daughter; but after a time I note an ancestral gesture, a customary expression, an incredible physical resemblance, a turn of phrase, and then I feel I am really talking with the father, or mother, who was my contemporary, or even the grandfather or grandmother. "It's been good seeing you, Thomas," I said at the end of one recent conversation. "I'm not Thomas," he replied. "I'm Robert. Thomas is my grandfather."

I have grown more tolerant because I see now I do not have all the time in the world. My feelings of humility deepen the more frequently I look around a room, or a dinner table, and acknowledge that I am the oldest person present. Likewise when my quirky subconscious sedulously whispers: Is this at last the day you sit down at your worktable and nothing at all comes out? "Ha, ha!" this diabolic interior traitor exclaims, "Nothing there at last!"

Time is a tricky fellow. Why is it that time passes so swiftly as we age? The moment has come for me to say that the one and only thing I am zealously intolerant of these days is the passing of time itself.

In childhood and youth, fool that I was, I wished time to pass quickly. I vividly remember sitting on a street curb at fifteen holding my baseball bat and beseeching the years to go by so that I could play ball in Yankee Stadium or Wrigley Field. In my twenties, in Chartres Cathedral, the waning sunlight filtering through the magnificent stained glass, I felt almost mystically immersed in time as *history*, in the ineluctable unfolding of the ancient human drama. In my thirties, I was half-oblivious to time, impatient as I was with matters of political and social reform. In my forties, I took most to my heart William Faulkner's dictum, "The past is never dead, it's not even past," past and present deeply linked for me in continuum. In my fifties, as I revisited New York City, I felt I had hardly made a ripple on that mutable place, and that time in my youth had somehow deceived me. Now, as I enter my sixties, I am beginning to view time as a difficult and most honored adversary.

As I put down these words on this page, I am pausing to gaze out the windows of my workroom. It is an unseasonably warm winter's forenoon in the deepest South. Down below me on the broad sloping lawn, I see the first robin bathing herself in a little puddle of water. In the distance, my beautiful wife is strolling languidly toward Purple Crane Creek, followed by my irascible cats Spit McGee, Mamie Harper, George W. Harper and Bessie Graham. The five of them are silently examining something in the grass. Could it be the first crocus? They seem so *together* there, caught for me in bittersweet frieze, in the belonging of the Lord's earth. They touch me deeply, and I implore: Stop, Time, you tricky fellow! Stop right now!

INDEX

Home and place, vii–x, xii–xiii, 13–17, 35, 74–75,
77, 89–91, 100–01, 102–03, 120, 123, 124–25,
150–54, 155–71, 173, 183, 202–04. *See also*
Family; Fathers and sons
House Un-American Activities Committee, 70
Humphrey, Hubert, 24

Intruders in the Dust (motion picture), 163
Ireland, 83, 157
Irving, Washington, *The Legend of Sleepy Hollow*,
148

Jackson, Miss., ix, 31, 42, 67, 68, 73, 74–75, 77–82,
84–85, 202
Jackson, Thomas "Stonewall" J., 6, 189
James Jones: A Friendship, 62
Jefferson, Thomas, 95, 117
Jitney Jungle, 75, 203
Johnson, Lyndon B., 21, 23–24, 189
Jones, Gloria, 46, 50, 184
Jones, James, 44, 46–51, 62–63, 64–65, 116–18;
From Here to Eternity, 46, 47, 49, 64; *The Pis-
tol*, 49; *Some Came Running*, 49; *They Shall
Inherit the Laughter*, 48; *The Thin Red Line*, 44,
46, 50; *Whistle*, 46, 48, 50, 51, 62, 63
Jones, Jamie, 47, 50, 116, 117
Jones, Jeff, 47, 48, 51
Jones, Kaylie, 50
Jumper, Fairy, 174

Kearns, Doris, 24; *Lyndon Johnson and the Ameri-
can Dream*, 23–24
Kefauver, Estes, 9
Kennedy, John F., 21, 24, 25, 157
Kennedy, Robert, 177, 191
King, Martin Luther, Jr., 28–29, 169
Knowles, John, 162, 184

Lamar Life building, 81
Land, significance of, 30, 39, 100–01, 113–14, 121,
155, 158–59, 161, 170
Laski, Harold, *The American Democracy*, 8–9
Lemuria Bookstore, 74
Leslie, John, 164–65
Library of Congress, 18, 19, 21
Lincoln, Abraham, 6, 7, 26, 71, 160
Little, John, 84–85
Long Island, N.Y., ix, 39, 42, 43, 45, 46, 50, 59, 62,
63, 111, 116, 117, 149, 155, 156, 162, 173. *See
also* Bridgehampton, N.Y.
Louisiana State University, 53, 56, 57

Mad magazine, 71
Mailer, Norman, 49
Manhattan. *See* New York City
Marrs, Suzanne, 75
Marx, Groucho, 19
Matthiessen, Peter, 62
Maxwell, William, 76
McCarthy, Eugene, 21, 22
McCrory, Mary, 62
Meade, Cowles (maternal great-great-great
uncle), 13
Mencken, H. L., 21
Meredith, James, 102, 103, 107, 109, 110, 157, 160,
168, 176–80
Mills, Wilbur, 61
Millsaps College, 34, 42, 84
Mississippi, 34, 36, 74, 80, 82, 102–10, 119, 121,
124–25, 155–71, 172, 174, 180. *See also* South
and Southerners
Mississippi Delta, 80, 100–01, 103, 105, 113, 121,
122, 147, 155, 156, 159, 168, 169, 178
Mississippi State College for Women, 80
Mississippi State Historical Museum, 75
Mitchell, Burroughs, 49, 50
Mobile, Ala., 59, 66, 67, 68
Morris, Celia Ann Buchan (first wife), 188–96, 201
Morris, David Rae (son), x, 15, 16, 37, 47, 113–14,
115, 116, 117, 148–50, 193–94, 195, 202
Morris, Henry Rae (father), 15, 16, 33–38, 100,
147, 154
Morris, Jan, *Oxford*, 128, 137–38
Morris, JoAnne. *See* Prichard Morris, JoAnne
(second wife)
Morris, Marion Weaks (mother), 15, 34, 35–36, 42,
154, 200
Morris, Nancy Stegall (paternal grandmother), 34
Morris, William (paternal grandfather), 34
Morris, Willie: ancestors and family of. *See* sur-
names Foote; Harper; Meade; Morris; Prich-
ard; Weaks
Mossolini, Gloria. *See* Jones, Gloria
Mullins, Roy Lee "Chucky," 54–57
My Dog Skip, vii–x

NAACP. *See* National Association for the Ad-
vancement of Colored People (NAACP)
National Association for the Advancement of Col-
ored People (NAACP), 105
Neshoba County, Miss., 28
New York City, 13–14, 39, 48, 49, 70, 72, 76, 81,

83, 111, 113, 114, 116, 155–56, 163, 166, 173, 188, 189, 191, 193–95, 201, 202–03, 204
New Yorker, 76
New York Times, 53, 68, 85, 95
New York Times Book Review, 83
Night-Blooming Cereus Club, 75
Nixon, Richard, 70
North and northerners, 23–27, 155, 157, 180
North Toward Home, viii, 202

Ole Miss. *See* University of Mississippi
Ole Miss magazine, 177, 180
Oliphant, Pat, 62
Oxford, Miss., 50, 67, 160–70, 178. *See also* University of Mississippi
Oxford University (England), viii, 8, 9, 35, 106, 127–43, 156, 173, 191, 197

Paris, France, 46, 50, 103, 116
Percy, Walker, *The Moviegoer*, 184
Perkins, Maxwell, 48–49
Perry, Ed, 158, 168
Peterhouse College, 83
Pets: Bessie Graham (cat), 204; Duke (dog), 147, 148, 154; George W. Harper (cat), 204; Ichabod Crane (dog), 112, 148, 149–50, 151, 152, 154, 192; Jimbo (dog), 147, 148, 154; Mamie Harper (cat), 204; Pete (dog), 39, 40, 150–54, 162, 172, 174, 182–83, 184; Sam (dog), 147, 148, 154; Skip (dog), vii, viii, 35, 36, 147–48, 151, 154, 202; Sonny (dog), 147, 148, 154; Spit McGee (cat), 204; Tony (dog), 147, 148, 154. *See also* Dogs
Philadelphia, Miss., 28, 29, 31
Players Club, 83
Poetry, 18–22
Politics, 3–6, 7–9, 10–12, 21, 23–27, 93, 94–99, 108–09, 155, 159–60, 164, 177–78
Porter, Katherine Anne, 77
Povich, Maury, 18, 22
Presidency, U.S., 3–6, 7; 1956 election, 3, 7–9; 1960 election, 9, 24; 1964 election, 23–24; 1968 election, 24; 1976 election, 23–27
Presley, Elvis, 9
Press, freedom of, 94–99
Price, Leontyne, 178
Price, Reynolds, 73, 74
Prichard Morris, JoAnne (second wife), ix, xiii, 67, 68, 127, 130, 136, 139, 143, 202, 204

Race relations, xi, 5, 14, 15, 20, 26, 28–30, 35, 102–10, 114, 119, 120, 124, 155, 157–61, 164–65, 167–71, 176–80
Racism. *See* Race relations
Raymond, Miss., 13, 14, 16, 123, 159
Reisman, David, 5
Religion, 23, 24, 26, 34–35, 53, 120
Rhodes, William "Billy," 203
Rhodes Scholarship. *See* Oxford University (England)
Richard Wright Medal for Literary Excellence, 77
Robinson, Ill., 46, 48
Roosevelt, Franklin D., 4, 5, 6, 70
Roosevelt, Theodore, 4
Royals, Tom, 84
Ruark, Robert, *Something of Value*, 37
Russell, Diarmuid, 81, 84

Sandburg, Carl, *Lincoln*, 11
Schwerner, Michael, 28, 29
Shaw, Adam, 59, 64
Shaw, Irwin, 59, 62, 65
Shelley, Percy B., 18–19
Shepherd, William "Muttonhead," 19
Sherwood, Jack, 62
Shivers, Allan, 94–95
Slaughter, John, 178
Sloan, Steven, 179
South and Southerners, 10–12, 21, 23–27, 34, 41, 45, 105–10, 119–26. *See also* Mississippi
Southerland, Trea, 55
Spencer, Elizabeth, 80–81
Sports, 36, 168, 178. *See also* Baseball; Basketball; Football
Stevens, Jack, 86
Stevenson, Adlai, 7–9
Storytelling, 14, 124, 157, 162
Styron, William, 21, 37, 44–45, 46, 49, 157, 184
Suddarth, Roscoe "Rocky," 141, 197, 198, 199
Switzer, Barry, 31

Taps, 64, 65
Tennyson, Alfred, "Ulysses," 183
Texas Observer, viii, 102, 108, 201, 202
Till, Emmett, 104
Town, living in small. *See* Home and place
Truman, Harry S., 4, 8

University of Mississippi, ix, xi, 34, 52–58, 59, 66, 102–08, 110, 124, 157–58, 160–62, 165, 166–67, 168, 170, 176–80. *See also* Oxford, Miss.